STAMP COLLECTING FOR PROFIT

Other book by Peter and Mary Harrison:
Coins and Banknotes for Profit

STAMP COLLECTING
FOR PROFIT

Peter & Mary Harrison

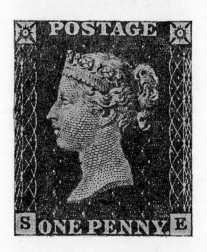

BARRIE & JENKINS
COMMUNICA · EUROPA

First published in 1979 by
Barrie & Jenkins Limited
24 Highbury Crescent, London N5 1RX

ISBN: 0 214 20510 X

Printed in Great Britain by The Anchor Press Ltd
and bound by Wm Brendon & Son Ltd
both of Tiptree, Essex

ACKNOWLEDGEMENTS

The authors wish to thank Stanley Gibbons Limited for permission
to reproduce the black and white photographs in this book. The
extract from *VAT Notice 712* is reproduced with the permission
of the Controller of Her Majesty's Stationery Office.

CONTENTS

1 GENERAL BACKGROUND

The first adhesive postage stamp in the world was the Penny Black, introduced on 6 May, 1840. The history of postage did not however start then. Postage dates back to many years before Christ. Ancient China and Persia had their own postal services. The Chinese had an efficient service, using couriers on horseback to deliver and collect messages. 'Post' is derived from the Latin *'positus'*, which was the name given to the places where postal messengers were stationed. The Romans had their own competent postmen who were part of the military organization. It was not until Edward I (1272–1307) that the king's messengers were used in England in an efficient and organized way, to deliver letters speedily. Much later, in England, it was left to the enterprising merchants to deliver mail (from the French *'malle'*) from place to place. This private postal service was frowned upon by the authorities, and the merchants took considerable risks in running it.

Henry VIII (1509–1547) introduced a manager for his postal service. This new appointment was the Master of the (King's) Posts, and Sir Brian Tuke was the first holder of the title. Oliver Cromwell (The Commonwealth 1649–1660) passed the first Post Office Act. In 1661, Colonel Henry Bishop held the position which was by this time renamed Postmaster General. Bishop brought in a hand-stamp which showed the day and month of posting. These stamps, called Bishop Marks, helped to speed up delivery. For the first time, mail had a printed mark showing the date of posting, and most of the postmen of that period were shown up to be inefficient and lazy, with no pride in the service they supplied.

Some twenty years later, a more efficient delivery service was put into operation in the areas of Westminster and the City of London. It was a better service than the one which exists today. For one penny, letters would be delivered on the day they were posted. The government didn't take kindly to this efficient private business enterprise, so it took it over and ran it itself. There was foolish talk at the time that the free-enterprise postal service known as Dockwra post was connected with a popish plot.

The volume of mail increased and it became necessary to arrange for long-distance delivery by stage coach and mail coach. By the late eighteenth century the stage-coach service was becoming highly organized. This eventually gave way to the transporting of all royal mail by the railways.

The sending of letters in 1830 was very expensive. To send a letter, one had to take it to a post office (or receiving house) and have it weighed, or the number of pages counted. The number of miles to be covered was taken into consideration when working out the total cost. Other factors, such as tolls on the roads en route to the destination, affected the postal costs. All these various amounts were added together, and usually made up a sum beyond the reach of the ordinary citizen. Therefore, before the Penny Black, postage costs were ridiculously high. The cost of sending a letter from London to Edinburgh was over 1s (one shilling). Postage was normally paid for by the recipient. It was not considered proper to prepay a letter being sent to a friend or relative; business letters, however, were normally prepaid. The post-office clerk would mark the cost on the front of the letter. If this was in red, it meant the letter had been prepaid; if the mark was in black, the postman had to collect the money from the recipient. All prepaid letters also had a red 'PAID' mark on them, which was added with an ordinary hand-stamp.

Rowland Hill

A headmaster from Kidderminster, Rowland Hill, thought the whole structure of the post office and postal collections and deliveries should be changed. In 1837 he published a pamphlet which advised the government on how they should organize post-office reform. He conceived the idea for prepayment of postage, apparently, after he came across a young woman who received a letter from her husband, opened it, read the message and then gave it back to the postman saying that she did not want it, and therefore wouldn't be paying the postage due. She had received her husband's message free, and Hill realized that, if the practice was widespread, it constituted a drain on the country's economy. Prepayment, in some way, was a must.

Stamps had been around for some time. The stamping section of the Board of Customs and Excise at Somerset House had been issuing adhesive labels/stamps since 1802, but it took Rowland Hill years to get the government to adopt a prepaid adhesive postage-stamp system for a countrywide postal collection and delivery service. He got no support whatsoever from the officials at the Post Office. A Colonel Maberly, who was the Secretary of the General Post Office, said that Hill's proposals were useless; the Postmaster General said that one penny was far too little to charge, and would result in a great financial loss.

Parliament thought differently, however, and in August 1839 a Bill called the Uniform Penny Postage Act was passed which made way for the introduction of penny postage. A fixed and regular rate for all postage was set, and all postage had to be prepaid. In December of the same year, a flat rate of fourpence was introduced, and then in January 1840 this was reduced to one penny. During the following four months, until the stamps were ready, the postage was prepaid before any letters would be accepted.

Penny Black and Twopence Blue

When the Penny Black and Twopence Blue first came onto the scene, the public were both dubious about having to lick the 'cement' and unfamiliar with the idea of removing small stamps from sheets. The stamps were not then perforated (this came about ten years later), and had to be cut with scissors or knife, or roughly torn off. The Post Office, therefore, issued publicity posters explaining how to go about 'affixing postage labels'. It didn't take long for the new form of prepaid adhesive stamps to be taken to the public's heart. In 1840 almost 170 million pieces of post were delivered, whereas in 1839 less than 80 million had been dealt with.

The Penny Blacks were made up into sheets of 240 (240 pennies to the pound), in rows of twelve. They were designed by Henry Corbould; the engravers were C. & F. Heath, and they were printed by the Anglo-American recess printers, Perkins, Bacon and Petch. As every stamp collector/investor knows, these early stamps are today worth a lot of money, but anyone who considered collecting such issues in the nineteenth century was looked upon as 'strange'.

The first dealer

The boy who, in 1856, started a collection of Penny Blacks in his father's chemist shop in Plymouth, started a stamp empire. He was Edward Stanley Gibbons, whose company now leads the field in stamp dealing and in the publishing of stamp catalogues and other books relating to every aspect of stamp collecting and dealing. Gibbons had a good business brain even as a boy. Those Penny Blacks he collected were resold to other collectors for 1/6d (one shilling and sixpence) each.

History's first stamp catalogue was published not by Gibbons, but in Paris in 1861. Other countries were slow to start their own adhesive-stamp productions. Although New York's City Despatch Post was using stamps less than two years after the British, it wasn't until 1847 that the United States officially took to adhesive postage stamps. Brazil was quicker off the mark with its famous 'Bull's Eye' issue in 1843. Various other countries, including Austria, Spain, France and Belgium, had adopted the idea by 1850. Some enterprising businessmen made small fortunes from the printing of stamps. One was Nicholas Seebeck, who printed South American stamps for nothing, but kept the plates and unsold stamps, from which he realized big profits.

2 GETTING STARTED AS A COLLECTOR/ INVESTOR

Buying stamps for profit means buying quality. Putting quality first means a sound investment for the future. Get to know your subject before investing a penny, and don't be taken in by all the loud colourful advertisements you may see in stamp magazines. Buy wisely. Dip your toe in before jumping in.

Philatelic societies

Join your local philatelic society. The address can be obtained from the British Philatelic Federation which publishes a handbook listing all the societies in this country, as well as some abroad.

The members of a well run society can expect expert advice through its publications, and, if the society operates a circulating packet, they may be able to purchase stamps. The society will also prove useful for exchanging stamps with fellow members, and for advising about which stamps are best for investment purposes. If the society is active and efficient, it will hold regular meetings during which experts give talks on all aspects of philately. At such meetings it is possible to pick up good investment stamps at bargain prices. A member might well sell off a stamp at far below the current market value if he is not particularly interested in it or in its country of origin.

The actual finding of stamps offers no real problem, as can be seen in the chapter entitled 'Buying'. The secret lies in the type of stamps you buy. The collector/investor must find quality stamps which are constantly rising in value. The best person from whom to get information about these is your local trusted dealer. Your philatelic society will put you onto the right dealers in your area. If you want to catch the bug of stamp collecting, then get to know the hobby side of it, which is in itself interesting: the design, historical and artistic points, and so on. Learn as much as you can about every aspect of philately so that you will gain the confidence you need in order to start investing in stamps.

Various aspects

The experienced collector/investor has to take into account various aspects when assessing values. These include the following:

(a) different watermarks
(b) different shades and slight variations in colour
(c) the difference between perforated and imperforate stamps which are similar in design
(d) the different plate numbers
(e) slight variations in design of similar stamps
(f) the true condition of the stamps

There are inexpensive ways in which you can dip your toe into stamp collecting. One way is to buy a cheap job lot, sort through them and then mount them in an album. This will give you some experience of handling stamps – help you to get the feel of your commodity. There is more to stamp collecting for profit than just buying a few chosen investment items, putting them away for a certain period of time, and then taking them down to the dealer to make a nice tidy profit. Investing in stamps means learning about them, caring for their condition and treating them with the respect they deserve. It is possible to be cold and calculating when it comes to investing, but even then, it is imperative to know about the stamps in your collection. The opposite extreme to the cold investor is the wide-eyed collector who takes out his stamps every night and just gazes in wonder at them.

Some collector/investors look upon the subject purely from the profit point of view, and spend only enough time studying stamps and mixing with other philatelists to ensure maximum financial gain. We feel this is a negative approach to the philatelic market. Surely it is wise to meet interesting collectors who have had years of experience, and are only too pleased to pass on their knowledge to the newcomer. You can never learn too much about philately. The businessman's proverb applies: 'Never go into anything without first learning all you can about it.'

Ground rules

For the person who wants to start from scratch, here are a few basic ground rules:

1. Join a philatelic society.
2. Read the books mentioned in the bibliography.
3. Contact dealers who have been recommended to you.
4. Attend auctions, but don't get carried away. Just watch at first.
5. Do buy packets of reasonably cheap lots. They could be from any part of the world, one country or continent. An 'All Reigns' issue should contain some Victorian stamps; or you may find stamps of one or more themes which could be the basis of a thematic collection, such as musicians, transport, birds, etc.
6. Make a close study of your job lot, and try out different arrangements in your album.
7. Check to ensure that (a) unused stamps have a complete backing of gum, and (b) that the used stamps have been cancelled with a light clear mark.
8. Perforated stamps should have all the teeth present and correct, and imperforate stamps should have good margins round the edges.
9. Never handle stamps. Always use tweezers, which are obtainable from any stamp dealer. Do not use domestic or cosmetic tweezers.
10. Buy a stamp colour chart and compare your own stamps with the colours and shades of those on the chart.
11. Obtain good magnifying apparatus, or a simple magnifying glass, and make yourself familiar with the finer points of printing and design. Also look for missing perforations and examine creases, etc.
12. Study stamp catalogues to help you identify stamps from different countries.

Stamp identification table

Lettering on the stamp	Country of origin
Acores	Azores
Afghanes	Afghanistan
A Payer – Te Betalen	Belgium

A Percevoir (franc and centimes value)	Belgium
A Percevoir (paras or milliemes value)	Egypt
Avisporto	Denmark
B (on Straits settlements)	Bangkok
Bani (on Austrian stamps)	Austrian occupation of Roumania
Bayern	Bavaria
Bayer Poste taxe	Bavaria
B.C.A.	British Central Africa
Belge or Belgique	Belgium
Braunschweig	Brunswick
C.C.C.P.	Russia
C.CH	Cochin China
C.E.F. (on German Colonies)	British Occupation, Cameroons
C.E.F. (on India)	China Expeditionary Force
Centesimi (on Austrian)	Austrian Occupation of Italy
Centimes (on Austrian)	Austrian Post Offices in Crete
Chiffre Taxe	France
Comunicaciónes	Spain
Confed. Granadina	Colombia (Granada Confederation)
Continente	Portugal
Correio (value in reis)	Portugal, Brazil
Côte Française des Somalis	French Somali Coast
CPBNJA	Serbia
Dansk Vestindien	Danish West Indies
Deutsche Reichspost	Germany
Deutsch Neu-Guinea	German New Guinea
Deutsch Ostafrika	German East Africa
Deutschösterreich	Austria
Deutsch Sudwestafrika	German South West Africa
Diligencia	Uruguay
DJ	Djibouti
Drzava or Drzavna	Yugoslavia
E.F.O.	French Oceanic Establishments
Eire	Republic of Ireland
Emp Franc	France
Equateur	Ecuador
España, Española	Spain
Estensi	Modena

Esti	Estonia
Établissements de l'Inde	French Indian Settlements
État Ind du Congo	Belgian Congo
Filipinas	Philippine Islands
Franco	Switzerland
Franco Poste Bollo	Neapolitan Provinces and Italy
Freie Stadt Danzig	Danzig
Frimaerke	Norway
G (on Cape of Good Hope stamps)	Griqualand West. Also used in Cape Colony
G and D (French Colonial)	Guadeloupe
G.E.A.	German East Africa (Tanganyika)
Giuba	Jubaland
G.P.E.	Guadeloupe
Grand Liban	Lebanon
Gross Deutsches Reich	Germany
Guinée	French Guinea
Guyane Française	French Guinea
Helvetia	Switzerland
Hrvatska	Yugoslavia
H.R.Z.G.L.	Holstein
I.E.F. 'D'	British Occupation, Mosul
Île Rouad	Rouad Island
Inde	French Indian Settlements
Island	Iceland
Karolinen	Caroline Islands
K.G.C.A. (on Yugoslavia stamps)	Carinthia (Austria)
K.K. Post. Stempel	Austria
K.P.H.T.H.	Crete
Kraljevstvo	Yugoslavia
K.u.K. Feld-post	Austrian military stamps
K.Wurtt. Post	Wurttemberg
La Georgie	Georgia
Land-Post	Baden
Latvija	Latvia
Lei (on Austrian)	Austrian Occupation of Roumania
Libia	Libya
Lieutuvos	Lithuania
L.Mc.L.	Trinidad
Losen	Sweden
Magyar	Hungary
MAPKA	Russia

Marruecos	Spanish Morocco
Mauritanie	Mauritania
Milit post Portomarke	Bosnia and Herzegovina
Modonesi	Modena
Moyen-Congo	Middle Congo
M.V.i.R.	German Occupation of Roumania
Napoletana	Naples
N.C.E.	New Caledonia
Nederland	Holland
Nederlandsch-Indie	Dutch Indies
N.F.	Nyasaland Field Force (Tanganyika)
Norddeutscher Postbezirk	North German Confederation
Nouvelle Calédonie	New Caledonia
NOYTA	Russia
N.S.B.	Nossi Be (Nosy-be)
N.S.W.	New South Wales
N.W. Pacific Islands	North West Pacific Islands (now New Guinea)
N.Z.	New Zealand
Oesterr, Oesterreich, Österreich	Austria
Oltre Giuba	Italian Jubaland
Orts Post	Switzerland
Pacchi Postale	Italy
P.C.C.P.	Russia
P.G.S. (on Straits Settlements)	Perak Service stamps
Piaster (on German)	German P.O's in Turkey
POCCIA	Russia
Pohjois Inkeri	Ingermanland
Porte de Conduccion	Peru
Porte de Mar	Mexico
Porto	Austria
Posta Cesko-Slovenska	Czechoslovakia
Postage	Great Britain
Poste Locale	Switzerland
Poste Vaticane	Vatican City
Post Stamp	Hyderabad
Preussen	Prussia
P.S.N.C. (Pacific Steam Navigation Co.)	Peru
R	Jind
R.F.	France and colonies
R.H.	Haiti (postage due)

R.O.	Eastern Roumelia
Sachsen	Saxony
S.H.	Schleswig-Holstein
S.H.S.	Jugoslavia
SLd.	Austrian Italy
S.O.	Eastern Silesia
Soldi	Austrian Italy
S.P.M.	St. Pierre and Miquelon
S. Thomas e Principe	St. Thomas and Prince Islands
S.W.A.	South West Africa
TAKCA	Bulgaria (postage due)
T.E.O.	Cilicia, Syria
Tjenste post frimaerke	Danish West Indies
Toga	Tonga
U.A.R.	United Arab Republic (Egypt)
U.G.	Uganda
Uku Leta	Hawaii
U.S.	United States
Venezia Tridentina (on Italy)	Italy (Trentino)
Y.C.C.P.	Ukraine
YKPAIHCbKA	Ukraine
Ykp H.P.	West Ukraine
Z. Afr. Republiek	S. African Republic (Transvaal)
Z.A.R.	Transvaal
Zeitungs	Austria, Austrian Italy
Zuid West Africa	South West Africa

The most important thing to do if you want to be successful as a stamp investor is to study the market. Don't rush headlong into buying stamps from, say, the Russian satellite countries because they have nice neat clear postmarks. These are probably C-T-O (Cancellation-to-Order) stamps, and are virtually worthless. If you check the gum on the back of the stamp and find it unused, this will confirm that the stamp has not been used for genuine postal service.

Many inexperienced collectors often wonder why their collections are valueless, while the collections of others are worth quite a deal of money. This is because the others have given some thought to the type of stamps they have bought. There is no secret of success here; it is simply a question of supply and demand. Stamps issued in the nineteenth century which were readily available and very common are probably in plentiful supply today, and are not therefore looked upon as a good investment. On the other hand, the Mauritius 1d stamp ('Post Office') is today worth thousands of pounds because only about a dozen are known to exist.

The question of demand is interesting, because it is rather complex. It is not always the rare stamp which is keenly sought after. While most rare stamps are worth a lot of money, there is no point in spending a fortune on a stamp which is too expensive for the average collector to buy. Your chances of selling it are slight. What you must do is to try to strike the correct balance between what you pay for the stamp, and the possibility of selling it at a high profit. The stamp must not, therefore, be too unusual and costly to fit into the average collection. Make it your business to find out what stamps are most popular with collectors and which can be sold at any time for a good profit.

Other investment hints

It is sometimes wise to stick to main issues. Some of the varieties which dealers often make a fuss about can cost a lot of money during a 'craze' period, but later when the craze passes, you may find that you are left with something nobody wants to buy. In that case the risk you took when buying the variety wasn't really worth it. If, however, the variety were to become listed in a catalogue, then the chances are that your original investment will be paid back many times over. It is often the case that errors which really stand out, such as the stamp being printed in a wrong colour, or with some misprint or mark, are usually catalogued as separate varieties and can be good investments. Always ask yourself this: Is it really possible for this variety to grow in value to a more appreciable amount than the ordinary straightforward issue? If, in your considered opinion, with or without advice from dealers and friends, the answer is 'no', then don't spend any extra cash on the variety, but stick to the main issue. Be sure to weigh up all the pros and cons carefully.

When working out investment potential, it is always wise to consider the number of stamps issued. You must bear in mind both the country of issue, and the face value of the stamps. A huge issue from a small country would not necessarily be a good investment, but an even larger issue from a country like Britain could be a good investment. It is a matter of relative values. The 7p or 9p stamp is issued in greater quantities than, say, the £1 stamp. The latter can in fact be sold to a dealer if it is in good condition and has a nice clear postmark. You could never sell him an ordinary 7p or 9p stamp. Some stamp collectors ask their relatives to send parcels to them for birthdays or Christmas, marked 'Please postmark carefully – Stamp Collector – Thank you'. The collector can then soak off the high-value stamps (50p, £1 etc.) and sell them at a profit – not a lot, perhaps, but he did get them for nothing.

When considering the investment potential of a stamp, always remember to differentiate between numbers of stamps issued and the number printed. Always go by the issued figures. The collector/investor then has to consider the number of stamps which would have been thrown away with the household rubbish, and those which would have been badly marked or torn.

A lot depends upon good judgment and common sense, with a peppering of good luck. This combination can turn an amateur collector into a successful collector/investor. Common sense means not putting all your eggs in one basket, and collecting a wide range of stamps. Some of the hottest tips for investors have turned out to be unsuccessful, whereas other stamps, which all the so-called experts didn't rate, have gone zooming up the investment charts. If you spread your investment across the board, and with advice from a good dealer, you should find a percentage of real winners, together with some slow climbers, and a few also-rans. Even the also-rans should be re-saleable, if they fetch only the price you paid for them; and they could rise just a little in value, over a period. So long as the prices don't fall, you should be pleased with this sort of investment.

Quality is of prime importance when spending your money; therefore only buy stamps in fine used or mint condition. Conditions in which stamps are sold include mounted mint, fine used, heavily mounted, part original gum.

First Day Covers (FDC) are worth more than ordinary mint condition stamps. However, it is always a good idea to back the horse both ways. Keep one mint and one fine used stamp (on an envelope) so that you are covered if the used stamp does become valuable. This can often happen with stamps issued by small countries where the postal service and traffic are small. The many mint stamps issued will, in this case, far outnumber the fine used stamps available on the philatelic market.

As a general rule it is better to stay clear of overprinted stamps. There are occasions when an overprint adds value to a stamp, but since the forger finds it comparatively easy to manufacture imitations, it is best to leave them alone – unless of course you are an expert on overprints. Another area of the philatelic world to avoid is the obscure, unique or near unique stamp. It is best to invest in the regular blue-chip stamp of which everybody is aware.

Probably the best way to make a real killing is to buy a series of 'sleepers'. These are stamps which are cheap today because nobody wants them, but which may increase greatly in the not too distant future. Anticipating which these are will take a great deal of detective work and judgment, and often give great pleasure in the process.

Countries which are always popular with philatelists are Great Britain, France, Eire, the Netherlands, Japan, Spain, Australia, New Zealand, Canada and the United States. Their stamps need not necessarily offer the greatest percentage increase in profits, but they will usually show a steady growth record. What the collector/investor must find is the country which will be most popular with stamp collectors in the near future, but as has been mentioned, it is easier and commercially more sound to spread the investment over several potential countries, or over a potential area, say, the Caribbean, or Scandinavia, Western Europe, southern Africa, Latin America (especially Mexico, Argentina, Peru and Venezuela). Any of these areas or countries is worth close investigation before deciding what your collecting/investing policy should be. Remember to be brave, and stick to your convictions; don't run with the crowd. The unpopular stamp issue of today could be the solid gold investment of tomorrow.

3 THE MAKE-UP AND CARE OF STAMPS

Paper
Stamps are made of different types of paper; these include Wove paper (most popular), Laid paper, Bâtonné paper, Granite paper, Quadrillé paper.

Wove paper
This has an even texture. The paper is used in books and newspapers as well as being widely used in the manufacture of adhesive postage stamps.

Laid paper
This has closely set lines which are either vertical or horizontal. The closely set lines are sometimes crossed at right angles by other lines which are widely set out.

Bâtonné paper
This has watermarked lines which are parallel and spaced apart. The paper is of a thin 'bank' type.

Granite paper
This contains small unbleached fibres which can be seen at the back of the stamp. Japan used this type of paper in stamp manufacture from 1922 to 1938. Switzerland has used the paper for stamps since 1882.

Quadrillé paper
This has a pattern of squares on it, which is produced by a series of crossed lines running across the paper. The French used it for the 1892 15 centime stamp, and other pictorial stamps from Obock and Djibuti.

The artist
The artist who designs stamps works on a scale several times larger than the stamp. He has to know which printing

process is to be used so that the drawing is given the correct treatment. The process could be recess printing, photogravure, typography or lithography. Each of these requires a different design technique. The recess printing process, for instance, can contain a lot of fine detail.

Engraving and printing
Recess printing
The design is engraved in reverse into the surface of a block of steel. This is then processed to produce numbers of replica plates. This form of printing process has been used for many stamps. It is thought of as the premier process.

Lithography (and offset lithography)
The old method was to print from limestone, but thin plates of zinc or aluminium are now used to good effect. Offset litho has been used successfully in Germany and other countries, and is photographically processed on to plates which are put on rotary press cylinders.

Photogravure
This is now the modern process used for multicolour high-speed runs on rotary presses.

Typography
This is a letterpress-type process. Electrotyping is now used to turn out the dyes in quantity. Typography is in fact opposite to the recess process; the design is in relief.

Watermark
The watermark is a pattern, letters or words produced in paper during the course of its manufacture. Watermarks can usually be seen by holding the stamp up to a light, or by putting it in a special watermark detector. This is a metal tray or black (porcelain) slab, and a very little trace of benzine is sometimes applied if the watermark is difficult to detect. It is important to note that photogravure stamps do not react well to the benzine treatment: there is danger of the colour running.

Gum

In the early days of stamp manufacture, gum was put on by hand. British typographed stamps were printed on pre-gummed paper. For stamps printed by the line engraving method (recess printing), the gum had to be applied after printing. This was because the paper had to be damp during printing in order to take the impression. Modern methods have made it possible for dry paper to be used, and therefore all the paper is now pre-gummed. Gum arabic and PVA are normally the adhesives used on stamps.

Perforations

The three main methods of perforating stamps are line perforation, comb perforation and harrow perforation.

Line perforation

This has a single line of holes either horizontally or vertically. The line of pins punches holes between each row down the sheet. The sheet is then turned round, and the process is repeated so that the lines are punched across the previous rows, at right angles.

Comb perforation

This method is used for perforating three sides of each stamp a row or more at a time. Several sheets can go through the comb in one sweep.

Harrow perforation

This is the process whereby stamps are perforated in one operation. The perforation is distinct from rouletting, which only cuts or pricks the paper. The perforation machine actually removes tiny discs of paper when it punches holes. Perforation succeeded rouletting in 1850 in Great Britain, and was invented by Henry Archer.

Care of stamps

Take great care of your stamps. They are extremely delicate and can be easily damaged. Careless handling can be costly, so safeguard your investment with all the equipment at your disposal. (See accessory chapter.) Always use tweezers when you study a stamp. Never pick up or handle a stamp with your fingers; no matter how clean and dry they are, some damage will be done to the stamp, even if it cannot be detected by the human eye. Get a good pair of philatelic tweezers (do not use the household variety) and start to use them as soon as you buy your first stamps. With regular use, you will become expert at sorting through your stamps, and tweezers are quicker for sorting than fingers anyway.

Being professional in your approach to stamp care is most important. If a dealer, or fellow collector/investor, finds that you have damaged a perforation or even slightly creased, torn or cut a stamp, he will not only doubt your philatelic ability, but will also worry about the quality of the rest of your collection. A potential purchaser must be certain that the stamps he is interested in have been well cared for. Never allow stamps to remain loose in an album, in a wallet or pocket. Remember to keep them away from strong sunlight. Stay well away from steam while handling them, for moisture of any kind is an enemy to stamps. They must be kept clean and dry.

When mounting stamps in albums, always use the best quality hinges. If you are dealing with unmounted mints then use Hawids (these are described in detail under 'Mounting'), or similar transparent strips or folders. The stamps can easily slide into place and are gripped adequately without any trouble. It is important to remember that not all transparent folders are ideal for stamp collections. Those which might transmit oil or moisture should be avoided. Remember to show your collection off at every available opportunity, not only because this will give pleasure but also because it will keep the stamps from becoming suffocated.

Always keep your collection in a cool and airy environment; stamps need air circulating around them. Beware of high heating temperatures and never put the collection in a cupboard near a cooker or radiator. Don't store it in the same place for long periods, but move it about.

If the collection starts to attain a high value and you entrust it to your friendly bank manager, make sure that his strong room is of the right temperature and humidity. Don't leave the collection locked up and forgotten about. You must take it out at regular intervals and inspect it, and remember to keep all albums and stock books on end. Never lay them flat; this puts pressure on the stamps. Keep all pages loose, and away from each other. Never store them tightly in plastic or polythene covers, but do put dust covers on your albums and make sure that no dirt or dust can get near them.

Just as in coin collecting, condition – and the maintaining of it – pays handsome dividends. The unmounted mint, in the finest possible condition, can fetch many times the price of a used stamp. Take a look at the 'comparative values' chapter and you will find tremendous differences between the SG selling prices of used and unused stamps. Stanley Gibbons states that prices in their catalogue are for stamps in fine average condition. Consider the differences in this following example:

Year	Stamp	Unused	Used
1840	2d blue	£1,750·00	£90·00
1841	1d red-brown	40·00	·80p
1855/57	4d red	950·00	50·00
1855/57	1s green	175·00	18·00
1862/64	9d bistre	250·00	30·00
1934	5s red	70·00	5·00

These prices have been taken from the Stanley Gibbons 'Collect British Stamps' Silver Jubilee edition (the twentieth edition). Although outstanding examples have been used to illustrate these differences, the trend is more or less continued throughout this particular catalogue.

True, mint and virginity are the investor's passwords to a successful financial pastime. Don't be satisfied with anything less, if it is at all possible to obtain the best. Some philatelists take things a little too far sometimes. 'Do not lick hinges', they say, 'because of the harmful bacteria on the tongue.' It makes you wonder if there are any purist collectors about who actually stop breathing when they inspect their collections. Or are they all dead?

Insurance

Insurance cover for all the stamps you buy is a must if you

intend to be a serious collector/investor. Your dealer will put you in touch with a company which operates philatelic insurance cover. Premiums can be quite reasonable, and if you're not happy with the first quotation, then shop around.

4 HOW TO ARRANGE YOUR STAMPS

Preparation

In order to show off your stamps to the very best advantage, you must prepare them properly. This means that each stamp will have to be neatly separated from its envelope without incurring any damage. Before you remove the stamp, however, you must check that the postmark itself is not in any way valuable. Bear in mind that the stamp is often worth much more if it is still attached to an envelope which bears an interesting postmark.

There are several methods of separating stamps from envelopes. Probably the most popular is termed 'floating'. To float a stamp, simply pour a little water into a saucer, then float the stamp and piece of envelope on top of the water with the stamp facing upwards. This allows the water to soak through the paper, making it easy to remove the stamp. *Take care that the stamp itself does not come into direct contact with the water.* If it should, damage might be caused which would reduce its value. When the envelope is sufficiently soaked, carefully peel it away from the stamp. It is important to remember that the *stamp should never be peeled from the envelope*; this again could result in damage.

Another method of separating stamps from envelopes is to use several sheets of thick blotting paper. Soak these with water, and then place the envelope and stamp on top, leaving them for a couple of hours or so. The envelope should absorb sufficient water to allow the stamp to be neatly separated. Most philatelic shops sell little gadgets called 'sweat boxes' which act in much the same way as the blotting-paper method.

Layout

Once you have prepared your stamps, the next step is to decide how you are going to display them in your album. Very elementary albums contain pages which are already printed up and undetachable. Because everything is mapped out, such albums pose no difficulty in displaying stamps, but neither is there any scope for individuality. Much of the appeal of philately lies in the sense of achievement in presenting an attractive and interesting collection, well arranged and neatly written up.

In order to arrange your stamps to your own particular layout, you will need an album with detachable pages. These come in many varieties and sizes with different forms of page attachments, such as clips, springs and pegs. Your album is entirely a matter of personal preference, but one with loose leaves that open out flat will probably have very light guide lines in the form of squares. These enable you to centre the stamps properly. Often the centre point of each stamp area is marked by a dot or a slight thickening of the vertical and horizontal lines at the point where they cross.

Before you start to mount your stamps, you would be advised to think about how you want the completed page to look. It is a mistake to stick stamps in willy-nilly; if you do this, the chances are high that they will later have to be taken out and re-entered. The less often you remove mounted stamps the better. They are exceedingly vulnerable to damage when they are being moved, and this can reduce your profit margins. Think carefully about the number of stamps you intend to place on each page, and about how you plan to place them. Normally, the name of the country of origin is displayed at the top of the page; each new country should be given a fresh page. Of course, there are exceptions to this rule, such as in specialist or thematic collections.

There are many ways of arranging the individual pages. Some experts say that it is best to start at the top, with stamps of the lowest face value, and work down until you enter the stamp of the highest value at the bottom. Others feel that the most important stamp of a set should be placed in the centre, and surrounded by the lesser stamps of its set. It is difficult to be dogmatic about arrangements, since this is a matter of taste and opinion. The best advice is to try several layout combinations before you mount, and to study the different effects, taking into account colour, number of stamps, size of stamps, etc.

Here are several possibilities that you might find helpful. Let us suppose that you have a set of nine stamps to place on a page. If you prefer the regimental approach, you might arrange them in three even rows of three, in straight

lines both vertically and horizontally, as in (A) below. Or
you might prefer to stagger the lines, in one of the several
ways illustrated.

```
(A)  1  2  3     (B)      1  2        (C)      1
     4  5  6            3  4  5              2     3
     7  8  9          6  7  8  9          4  5  6
                                           7  8  9

(D)  1  2  3     (E)  1  2  3
     4  5  6            4  5
       7  8          6  7  8
          9                9
```

Mounting

To mount your stamps, you will require a pair of tweezers
and some hinges, which are small pieces of paper gummed
on one side. These are stuck on to the page and also on to
the stamp, leaving the stamp as free as possible but still
securely attached to the page.

Fold one-third of the hinge over, with the gummed part
outward; then make a neat crease across the fold. Wet the
folded one-third and, using the tweezers, carefully place the
reverse of the stamp on the wet part of the hinge so that the
two are joined just below the top line of perforations. It is
important to place the stamp on the hinge accurately. If
you do not, you will run up against trouble when trying to
inspect the reverse after it has been mounted. You may also
find that the hinge will show over the top of the stamp if it
is placed too near the top perforations.

Once the stamp is attached to the hinge, make sure that
you know exactly where on the page it is to be entered.
Then wet the remaining two-thirds of the hinge and carefully stick this to the page. To ensure that the stamp is
properly centred, make use of the horizontal and vertical
guide lines. It takes about an hour for the hinge to dry
thoroughly, and during this period the stamp should not be
touched.

When entering your second stamp, be sure to allow plenty
of space between it and the first. Not only does a page
cluttered with too many stamps look unsightly, but it leaves
insufficient room to write in the details of each stamp, and
this only adds to the muddle. A rough guide is to allow at
least four squares between each stamp in a row, and about

six squares between the rows. Remember to leave extra space around the margins of the page, especially on the outer right- and left-hand margins where you handle the pages in order to turn them.

If you have a very large stamp, or one of an unusual shape or of particular interest, you might want to devote half a page to displaying it properly. Some people even allow an entire page for a single truly remarkable stamp. You may come across stamps which have been mounted while still attached to their envelopes. This is undoubtedly because there is some importance attributed to the postmark. If so, stamp and envelope are often given a whole page.

If you have mounted a set of stamps on one page, and one stamp is of particular interest, you can draw attention to it by surrounding it with a coloured border. This shows it off without taking too much space. However, guard against using borders too often, or they will cease to be effective.

Some people surround their mounted stamps with designs or squiggles. These achieve nothing but to destroy the main purpose of an album, which is to show off stamps, clearly, in plenty of space and without diversions. Many albums come with black pages, which provide a good contrast to the colour of the stamps and thus help them to make maximum impact.

Some people now insist upon stamps being unmounted, a practice which came into fashion in the 1960s. If you wish to cater for this 'unmounted only' section of the market, you can still keep your stamps in an album, by means of Hawid strips. These are pocket-type folders which are available in various sizes, some even big enough to accommodate entire blocks of stamps. Each folder, fitted with a transparent front and a back usually of black, is attached to the page by the normal mounting process. The stamp is then placed in the pocket where it can be seen clearly without any further handling. This is an excellent method of protecting valuable stamps, even though they may have been mounted by a previous owner. The minimum amount of handling is required to keep the stamps in the best possible condition.

Writing up

Each entry in your album should have some form of explanation written beside it. It is always a good policy, especially for the beginner, to keep the writing as brief as possible, except perhaps in the case of specialist or thematic collections. Normally, the country of origin should be entered at the top of the page. This can be done by hand, or by means of small typewritten labels, or you might prefer to buy gummed tabs with the names of countries printed on them, which you can obtain from your local stamp shop.

Underneath each stamp you should write the date of issue and the title of the set (if there is one). If for some reason, as in thematic presentations, you have stamps of different countries on the same page, then the country of origin should be entered under each stamp. If there are any special points of interest, such as the number of perforations, the watermark, the reason for the issue, e.g. the Olympic Games, etc, then these should be mentioned in the write-up. Do not enter the catalogue price, or any other catalogue details.

If you are dealing with specialist stamps, you will be required to provide more information, such as the artist's name, design details, etc; but words should be kept to a minimum, in order not to take away from the impact of the stamp itself. It can be interesting, in specialist or thematic arrangements, to use a certain amount of descriptive art work in the form of diagrams or maps. This should not be attempted, however, unless you feel confident of producing a neat job. It is possible to buy small paper arrows which are used for drawing attention to details of interest on stamps. These are stuck on to the page (never to the stamp) and the point of the arrow is allowed to overlap the stamp.

When entering the information, the best rule is to use your normal style of handwriting – if it is legible. This adds your own personal touch to the arrangement. If, however, you feel that your handwriting leaves something to be desired, you can either print the information in neat block capitals, or type it on labels or on small sheets of paper, which you can then attach to the page. Some people type the information directly on to the page, but this method is not recommended. Since the wording must be typed before the stamps are mounted (they would be damaged during the typing if they were mounted first), it is easy to mis-calculate the relationship between the words and the ultimate position of the stamp. This can create problems when it comes to mounting.

Specialist and thematic arrangements

Layout is particularly important with specialist and thematic arrangements. The nature of these subjects offers great scope for making striking presentations. Remember, however, that only details directly related to the stamp should be entered. For instance, if you were dealing with music, it would be of interest to enter the date of issue, the composer's name, the artist, designer, engraver, the reason for the issue, etc. You might want to include a photograph of the subject, or perhaps a map showing his birthplace, and you could name a couple of his most famous works. But it would be a mistake to insert an entire musical score, or write out his life story.

In thematic arrangements, the theme should be entered at the top of the page. If you have stamps of several different themes, they should be clearly sectioned off from each other. Thematic collections can be assembled on a wide range of subjects (see Chapter 5, 'Stamps to Buy'). Some people, for instance, collect stamps which contain printing errors; others collect stamps with changes of shade of colour in the same set. These all need to be explained by drawing lines towards the areas of the stamp on which the peculiarity exists, or by affixing the small paper arrows mentioned earlier.

Removing stamps

If you have to remove a stamp from a page of your album, it should peel off fairly neatly, provided it has been pro-perly mounted. First of all, remove the hinge and the stamp from the page. Then very carefully peel the hinge away from the stamp. This is easier to accomplish if you turn the stamp over so that the reverse is facing upwards, than the other way round.

If you have just completed mounting a set of stamps and you realize that one stamp has been placed wrongly, you must not attempt to remove the stamp until the hinge is completely dry. This takes about an hour, as we said earlier. Then follow the instructions above.

Beginners are often puzzled about how to deal with missing stamps. They might have a set with only one stamp missing, and can't decide whether to leave a gap on the page in the hope that they will soon obtain the stamp, or whether to enter the rest of the set without leaving a space. On the one hand, the gap draws attention to the fact that there is a stamp missing; on the other, if no gap is left, and the missing stamp is suddenly acquired, the entire page may have to be rearranged to make space for it.

Perhaps the best advice is to arrange the page in such a way that the missing stamp can be easily entered without having to move the existing mountings. This is not a serious problem if the missing stamp is from either of the extremes – the one with the lowest value, or the highest. However, this is usually too convenient to be true. More often than not, the missing stamp is from the body of the set, which creates an awkward problem. Nevertheless, it is sometimes possible to arrange the rows of stamps so that the gap is either at the start of the finish or a row, and thus not too disturbing to the eye.

The idea, of course, is to camouflage the gaps. Under no circumstances, therefore, should you write up details for the missing stamp or make any reference to it. This will only draw attention to the fact that your page is not complete.

One last word on the subject of removing stamps from pages of the album. This is comparatively simple to do, if you use card mountings, or mats, as they are sometimes known. These are small square cards, slightly larger than the stamp, on which the stamp is mounted in the normal way. The card is then mounted on the page with either one or two hinges. If, later, the stamp has to be removed, or moved to a different section of the album, the entire mat comes off the page. Then it is re-entered using a fresh hinge. This protects the stamp itself from the damge that can be caused by being mounted too many times.

5 STAMPS TO BUY

If you are to make a success of stamp collecting for profit, it is essential that you buy your stamps wisely. Think in terms of investment rather than collection. However pleasant it may be for a collector to acquire a stamp which he has long searched for, to complete a page, he will not necessarily make much of a profit from the acquisition. On the other hand, a person who buys stamps purely with the profit angle uppermost in his mind will almost certainly make money on his transactions.

Knowledge

Before setting out to buy stamps it is advisable to study the current market values. It is most important to know just how much any particular stamp is worth. If you feel that you need a bit of moral support, or a trusted second opinion, ask a friend who has knowledge of market trends to accompany you.

Auctions

If you yourself are well acquainted with the current market values of the stamps you want to buy, and do not wish to trade through a dealer, then you could consider buying at an auction. If you are lucky, you could end up with a real bargain. However, there are certain pitfalls of which the inexperienced bidder should be wary. For instance, if the bidding for a particular set of stamps goes well above the figure you had expected it to fetch, you will have to decide whether there is a genuine reason, or whether this is merely the result of several inexperienced buyers willy-nilly out-bidding each other.

When you inspect the lots you are interested in, look out for errors, and so forth. These could well mean profits for you when you re-sell.

Be on the lookout, also, for similar types of lots at auction sales. When these are offered, watch carefully to see how many different people bid. Once you have more or less established the number of bidders interested in these similar lots, you will note that, as successive lots are sold, the number of bidders gradually falls, until perhaps only one or two remain. Keep track of how many of the sets are left to be disposed of and try, where possible, to make a serious bid for the second last set. Do not go out actually to buy this set, but let it go to the other bidder (with luck, the last person interested in the similar sets, apart from yourself). When the final set is offered, then you stand a good chance of buying it for a fraction of the cost of the first set sold. You will have managed to secure a good bargain because all the other interested bidders had already made their purchases.

Another tip is to go to a large auction and reserve your bids until the sale is almost over. By that time, most of the high bidders will either have bought what they required, or spent their quota of money.

New issues

Every so often new stamps are issued which can be bought at your local post office or from the postal administrations of countries abroad. Sometimes only a certain limited number of these new stamps are issued, which may make them difficult to come by. There are, however, many dealers who buy stamps for commission. Since such dealers will probably be acting for several clients, their orders will be large enough to place them in the necessary category for obtaining new stamps which have a restricted issue, or, as known in the trade, a limited release. It is worthwhile getting to know a reputable dealer, because limited releases of some countries can be purchased only as part of a sizeable order for various other stamps. Normally the dealer is paid in advance by the client; in addition to his percentage of commission, he may charge a handling fee to cover such expenses as postage and overseas telephone calls.

C-T-O

You may come across stamps which are catalogued as C-T-O. These letters stand for Cancellation-to-Order, and this means that they have been specially postmarked by the authorities, so that they can be offered to collectors and dealers as used stamps. They are usually sold at a price lower than the face value, and are often used for making up small packets of stamps of the type collected by children. When some countries issue new stamps they often dispose of the older issues by cancelling them to order.

Specializing

When you are setting up your collection you should first of all make up your mind on what type of stamps you intend to concentrate. It could be that you will decide to specialize in stamps of one particular country or continent. Or perhaps you would like to establish a name for yourself in connection with stamps which have been designed along a certain theme. This is called thematic philately and it affords enormous scope, since the number of stamps which come under a particular heading is not restricted by geographical or historical factors. The possibilities are vast when you consider the many different designs used on stamps the world over. The most popular themes are flowers, animals, birds, ships, motor cars, trains, buildings, musical instruments, religious motifs, trees and insects. Many people specialize in commemorative issues, and in errors and varieties.

Dealers

Many dealers run a service whereby they represent clients at auction sales. This can be very helpful to people who are new to the business and who may not have much experience of bidding. The dealer is given an amount of money by the client, and a rough idea of the type of stamps required. Sometimes, however, the client leaves the question of what to buy entirely to the discretion of the dealer.

Shop around before you make a final decision about the dealer with whom you will trade. Try to find one who is well established and has been operating for many years. The fact of business longevity must prove not only that he is reliable and trustworthy, but also that he knows his trade. Most good dealers will be pleased to let you browse through their catalogues and will be quite happy to let you have the occasional bargain. They undoubtedly look upon this as an incentive for further transactions. The dealer will provide you with all your normal catalogue stamps and he can also obtain new issues for you, as well as acting both as your auction representative and general advisor. Many dealers have forms on which you can list all the stamps you are looking for. This is called the 'wants list'. As the dealer acquires the stamps listed, he will send them on to you. Most dealers are also quite happy to send stamps out on approval to their customers.

Circulation packet

Another method of obtaining stamps is by means of the circulation packet. This is a system in which a packet, or box, containing booklets of stamps (all priced) is passed round the members of a philatelic club or society. The system, which is often also referred to as the circulating exchange packet, works as follows. The packet is sent out by the society's organizer, to the first person named on a previously compiled list. If he finds stamps that he wants to buy, he removes them from the booklets, sends a remittance for their value to the organizer, and sends the packet on to the second name on the list. Thus it works its way through the entire list. When the last person removes the stamps of his choice, he sends the box back to the organizer. The next time the packet is circulated, the list is altered so that the person who was previously at the top is at the bottom; the person who was second becomes first, and so on. This ensures that everyone gets a fair chance of having the first and widest choice.

You can sell stamps as well as buy them this way. Club members mount stamps they wish to dispose of (unwanted stamps from mixed lots, for instance) on to the pages of the booklets for circulation. When the circulation packet is returned to him, the organizer pays the people whose stamps have been sold. Usually a small commission is charged, to help cover the costs of postage, booklets, etc. Should there be any money left over once all expenses are cleared, this goes towards the club funds.

Best buys

It is difficult to predict best buys as far as new issues are concerned, but it is always worthwhile to invest in the classics, particularly the first issues of stamps of countries before 1900. These can be fairly expensive, but they are considered a sure-fire investment. Their catalogue prices rise each year, and it is logical to assume that as time goes on they will automatically become more and more precious: some will inevitably be lost, and this will make them even more rare.

When buying the more expensive classics, make sure that you pay attention to condition. This could mean the difference between making an excellent profit, and realizing only a fair exchange. If, therefore, you find yourself faced with a choice of buying many classics in poor condition and buying one single classic in excellent condition, then choose the latter. Also, if you are offered two classic stamps, one at a considerable reduction because it is in poor condition and one in superb condition at a higher price, do not be tempted into buying the cheaper stamp. It will be well worth it to pay the higher price and be confident that you have a winner. Some dealers have a guarantee mark which is shown on the reverse of the more expensive stamps, and attests that the stamp is genuine.

6 SELLING

A lot of people are surprised to learn that 60 million Penny Blacks were printed, and that some of these are being sold for just a few pounds. These 'cheaper' Penny Blacks will rise in value more slowly than the more sought after expensive types. The collector will recognize a more expensive Penny Black by examining it for a plate number and checking this against his list. Generally speaking, stamp investing is like any other business; you have to speculate to accumulate. To illustrate the point, look at the following comparative values: in 1975 the SG selling price for the 1840 unused Penny Black (SG Cat. No. 2) was £200, and in 1977 the SG selling price for the same stamp was £450. A difference of £250 in two years! A used Penny Black in 1975 was £15, and in 1977 it had doubled to £30, a difference of £15. These figures show that the collector/investor with money to spend is the man who will profit most.

Judgment

The collector/investor who has acquired British pre-1914 stamps in mint condition will be able to sell his collection for a handsome profit, if he bought the stamps at a reasonable price in the first place. In the 'comparative prices' chapter, you will see that up to the 1913–18 issue of King George V stamps, the price increases between 1975 and 1977 were substantial – over 100 per cent in some cases. The 1912 to 1922, 1924 to 1926, and subsequent issues, show a levelling off in values and price increases.

Successful selling is a question of astute judgment. Knowing when to sell is the secret of profitable philately. The World Cup Victory stamp of 1966 is a typical example of selling at the right time. This 4d, multicoloured stamp is priced at 12p unused, 25p used and 90p FDC in the SG 'Collect British Stamps' Catalogue of 1977 (twentieth edition). Those collector/investors who fought to buy the World Cup winner stamps on 18 August 1966 have a potential profit of approximately 10p on each unused stamp in their possession. Some collectors have sheets of these stamps locked away waiting for the right day to sell. They've missed it. The right day to sell was the day of issue, immediately after they had purchased the stamps. There was an atmosphere of 'auction fever' bordering on hysteria when they were issued. At most post offices there were long queues and all the stamps were bought up within hours. Later the same day, dealers were offering, and getting, 25p and more for the World Cup winner stamps. They couldn't get enough of them, and shrewd collector/investors sold their sheets of the 4d stamps and made a lot of money. Later, as more and more of the stamps became available through dealers, the urgent need to acquire a fourpenny one diminished. The bottom had dropped out of this particular market and an awful lot of people missed the boat.

Market study

Whether you are selling all your stamps, or only some of them, you must study the market. You may want to sell some and, with the capital acquired, buy others. In this way you can improve your collection without dipping into your own financial resources. There is a technique to selling which is acquired with experience. You must not accept less than the lowest figure you have set, whether you are selling privately to a dealer, or via an auction. If you are offered a low sum, don't be downhearted; just take your collection home and try again another day. Try other collectors, other dealers, other auction firms. There are plenty around. If you have the quality stamps which are in demand, sooner or later you are going to get the price you want.

Turning your stamps back into cash will probably appeal to your business instinct. It certainly did in the case of the collector who was casually talking over business with his favourite dealer, one sunny day in London a few years ago. The dealer spotted a very well-known philatelist in his shop, and rudely left the collector to talk to him. The collector had to wait a very long time before he was rejoined by the now elated dealer. The collector hid his annoyance, smiled and produced a 'rare' bottle-green stamp for the dealer to examine. The dealer put the stamp through all the usual tests and was so impressed that he offered the collector twenty pounds. The collector pocketed the money and said 'I just bought that stamp from your assistant for fifty pence, while I was patiently waiting for you.' Variations of this story have been enjoyed by philatelists for some time, and this one does have an element of truth about it. A stamp in the 'chorus line' one minute can be the 'star' of the show the next.

Selling to the right person at the right time is important. Don't do what the collector fresh up from the country did. After tut-tutting and um-umming over the collection, the dealer made an offer of fifty pounds. The stamps were worth many times that amount, but the collector's blind faith in dealers persuaded him to accept the figure. The collector should, of course, have obtained a proper valuation before he considered selling, and he should have chosen a reputable dealer, preferably one belonging to a philatelic trade association. It is also worth noting that more than one employee in a stamp-dealer's shop has been known to purchase a good collection for a pittance and then sell it for a big profit to another dealer, thereby cheating both the collector and his employer. The principals of stamp-dealing companies have clamped down on this of late, so it is hoped that you will not encounter the problem, but it is important that you are aware of it.

The best possible advice to give for selling stamps is to know the market. You must mix with all the dealers and collector/investors to find out who is after what. A selection of British classics being offered to one dealer might bring a valuation only fifty per cent of that offered by someone who is desperately anxious to acquire those classics.

Advertising

Advertising in the various philatelic magazines can sometimes prove successful. Write or phone the magazine you want to advertise in and ask for their latest rates. When compiling your advertisement pay special attention to layout. Study current advertisements to see how the experts set out their displays. The established dealers have been advertising for a long time and they know how to appeal to the buying public. Decide which stamps you want to include in your advertisement so that you can work out the space you need, and then get the valuations right. If you charge the same or more than the established firms you are not likely to receive many if any orders. A reduction of five or ten per cent will entice the customers and shouldn't hit your margins too much. However, do not forget to take into account the cost of the advertisement. A loss leader, or cheap offer, could lead to an avalanche of replies. This is not necessarily a good idea; it can waste both your time and money – in sending back remittances, or in replying to say that you've sold the stamp to someone else. It is advisable not to make advertisements open-ended. The offer should be for a stated period only: offer closes in ten, fourteen or twenty-one days, or by a fixed date. Remember to state all descriptions fairly and accurately. Failure to do this could render you liable under the Sale of Goods Act, or Trade Descriptions Act.

Auctions

A stamp which is rare or in fashion will invariably do well at an auction. It is important to know the true valuation of the stamp or stamps you are selling, and to set a reserve price accordingly. Remember that commission has to be paid to the auctioneers whether or not you complete the sale. If you are selling an album collection, it is important to show that the stamps have been well cared for, and all must be written up in a legible and professional manner. The auctioneer will make sure that all the relevant information is passed on to possible customers via the catalogue, but it will do no harm to check the details he will distribute and the copy he will use. Do not have any rubbish items in the album – only saleable goods of the finest quality.

If you have stamps which are in vogue, then you will probably be lucky enough to have dealers bidding against other dealers and also against eager collectors. Stamps in demand can bring very high prices. If you have what the buyers are looking for, then auction fever could push the price up to well above your highest hopes. But unless you need cash quickly, do not accept less than the lowest figure you had set for yourself in advance. You have spent time and money in building up your stamp-investment collection. Why let someone else have it for next to nothing? That buyer will probably make a nice profit at the next auction, or via a dealer or advertisement.

Be that as it may, you must bear in mind that the next

chap wants a fair profit too. For instance, if you enter your stamps for sale on a rising market, the chances are that you will get a quick and satisfactory sale, because the purchaser will be able to re-sell the stamps to his advantage. The unsuccessful end to that story would be to get too greedy and wait too long, by which time the market for your particular stamps could be on the downwards slope.

There are numerous collectors who put the artistic and hobby side of philately before profit-making, and a lot of them can be very vocal about this objective. We would be very surprised if, should they have to sell their collections, they were not disappointed to see their beloved hoards going at auction at knock-down prices. Many a purist, however, in these circumstances, learns to his delight that he has purchased wisely over the years. When he hears the bidding at an auction getting higher and higher, you can bet your bottom dollar that he will be giving himself a metaphorical pat on the back, and be pleased to reap a handsome profit. And well he might be pleased; he has earned his reward. Sadly, however, the money in the bank will never compensate for the dearly missed collection which he had nursed and nurtured.

Dealing with dealers

If, after gaining knowledge and experience, you are able to assess the value of your collection, don't be too disappointed if a dealer offers you a lot less than your asking price. If you have done your homework properly on the valuation, and you have stamps which are popular, you will eventually find a dealer who wants them. If he has a client waiting for the stamps you are offering, thereby assuring him of a quick sale, he may even offer you your asking price. The thing is to bide your time and wait for the right dealer.

7 COMPARATIVE VALUES

We are indebted to Stanley Gibbons Publications Limited for allowing us to quote the following comparative prices as featured in their publications *Collect British Stamps* – 1975 and 1977. The prices quoted are selling prices at the time each book went to press. The first list of prices comes from the sixteenth edition (1975), and the second list comes from the twentieth edition (1977).

As previously mentioned, the prices of the older stamps, in unused condition, have risen appreciably more than those of the modern issues, and it is important to remember that the following lists should be taken only as an example of price variations on some British stamps of 1840 to 1975. The list includes a few plate numbers, but it does not include watermarks, errors, missing phosphors, variations, graphite-lined issues, or any other factors which could have a bearing on the price of a stamp. It cannot be over-stressed, therefore, that a thorough knowledge of stamps is necessary before contemplating the setting up of a philatelic business. There are numerous pointers which affect selling prices. For example, an 1858/70 1d red printed on plate number 78 and in unused condition is priced at £4·00, whereas a 1d red printed in the same period and in the same condition is priced at £11,000. The plate number in this case is the one before, number 77.

The catalogue numbers listed are per the Stanley Gibbons catalogue.

SG Cat. No.	Date	Stamp	1975 Unused £	1975 Used £	1977 Unused £	1977 Used £
2	1840	1d black	200·00	15·00	450·00	30·00
5	1840	2d blue	500·00	55·00	1,700·00	90·00
8	1841	1d red-brown	14·00	0·40	40·00	0·80
14	1841	2d blue	130·00	6·00	275·00	12·00
17	1854–57	1d red-brown	12·00	40·00	40·00	1·00
19	1854–57	2d blue	110·00	5·00	350·00	9·00
36	1854–57	1d red	50·00	3·50	175·00	10·00
36a	1854–57	2d blue	225·00	15·00	700·00	40·00
48 pl. 4.	1858–70	½d red	4·00	75·00	11·00	1·25
48 pl. 9.	1858–70	½d red	120·00	20·00	350·00	55·00
51 pl. 1.	1858–70	1½d red	25·00	4·00	90·00	7·00
51 pl. 3.	1858–70	1½d red	16·00	2·50	45·00	4·50
62	1855–57	4d red	400·00	18·00	950·00	50·00
64	1855–57	4d red	190·00	12·00	500·00	40·00
66a	1855–57	4d red	65·00	4·00	140·00	9·00
70	1855–57	6d lilac	50·00	4·00	130·00	10·00
72	1855–57	1s green	75·00	8·00	175·00	18·00
76	1862–64	3d red	55·00	12·00	160·00	28·00
82	1862–64	4d red	40·00	3·75	120·00	8·50
84	1862–64	6d lilac	45·00	·50	140·00	10·00
86	1862–64	9d bistre	85·00	14·00	250·00	30·00
90	1862–64	1s green	65·00	7·00	175·00	15·00
92 pl. 4.	1865–67	3d red	55·00	4·50	140·00	11·00
94	1865–67	4d vermilion	20·00	3·00	65·00	7·00
97	1865–67	6d lilac	40·00	3·75	120·00	9·00
98	1865–67	9d straw	100·00	30·00	275·00	70·00
99 pl. 1.	1865–67	10d brown	not known	2,250·00	not known	5,000·00

45

SG Cat. No.	Date	Stamp	1975 Unused	1975 Used	1977 Unused	1977 Used
101 pl. 4.	1865–67	1s green	£ 40·00	£ 3·75	£ 110·00	£ 8·50
103 pl. 5.	1867–80	3d red	20·00	2·50	60·00	4·00
103 pl. 4	1867–80	3d red	45·00	6·00	120·00	17·00
104	1867–80	6d lilac	35·00	40·00	160·00	10·00
109 pl. 9	1867–80	6d mauve	30·00	3·00	90·00	7·50
109 pl. 10	1867–80	6d mauve	not known	2,750·00	not known	4,500·00
111 pl. 4	1867–80	9d straw	50·00	8·00	160·00	24·00
112	1867–80	10d brown	65·00	10·00	225·00	24·00
117	1867–80	1s green	40·00	1·25	90·00	2·25
119	1867–80	2s blue	110·00	8·00	300·00	20·00
121 pl. 1.	1867–80	2s brown	550·00	120·00	1,400·00	275·00
123	1872–73	6d brown	35·00	2·75	90·00	6·00
125 pl. 12.	1872–73	6d grey	25·00	4·25	120·00	12·00
126	1867–83	5s red	200·00	16·00	450·00	40·00
128 pl. 1.	1867–83	10s green	1,250·00	90·00	4,750·00	200·00
129 pl. 1.	1867–83	£1 brown	1,500·00	140·00	5,750·00	350·00
134 pl. 4.	1867–83	5s red	450·00	65·00	1,400·00	125·00
135 pl. 1.	1867–83	10s green	1,750·00	120·00	5,750·00	300·00
137 pl. 1.	1867–83	£5 orange	700·00	200·00	1,600·00	425·00
139	1873–80	2½d mauve	18·00	2·25	65·00	6·00
141 pl. 17.	1873–80	2½d mauve	30·00	10·00	120·00	24·00
142	1873–80	2½d blue	15·00	1·25	50·00	2·50
143	1873–80	3d red	18·00	1·75	65·00	4·50
145 pl. 13.	1873–80	6d pale buff	not known	575·00	not known	900·00
147	1873–80	6d grey	18·00	2·50	55·00	5·50
150	1873–80	1s green	22·00	4·00	60·00	7·00
150 pl. 14.	1873–80	1s green	not known	2,750·00	not known	5,000·00

No.	Date	Description				
151 pl. 13.	1873–80	1s brown	85·00	16·00	275·00	38·00
152	1873–80	4d vermilion	70·00	16·00	160·00	35·00
153	1873–80	4d green	30·00	7·00	90·00	18·00
154 pl. 17.	1873–80	4d brown	30·00	8·00	150·00	22·00
156 pl. 1.	1873–80	8d orange	40·00	8·00	150·00	20·00
157	1873–80	2½d blue	14·00	0·75	45·00	1·50
158	1873–80	3d red	16·00	1·75	55·00	3·75
165	1880–81	½d green	0·90	0·30	4·50	0·80
169	1880–81	4d indigo	35·00	5·00	100·00	12·00
172	1881	1d lilac	15·00	5·00	35·00	12·00
179	1883–84	2/6d lilac	32·00	7·00	100·00	16·00
181	1883–84	5s red	40·00	7·00	140·00	22·00
183	1883–84	10s blue	65·00	18·00	250·00	65·00
185	1884	£1 brown	850·00	80·00	2,250·00	225·00
186	1888	£1 brown	1,400·00	130·00	5,000·00	375·00
191	1883–84	3d lilac	10·00	3·00	30·00	8·00
195	1883–84	9d dull green	50·00	30·00	160·00	55·00
197	1887–1900	½d vermilion	0·10	0·05	0·30	0·15
200	1887–1900	2d green and red	2·50	0·50	6·00	1·25
209	1887–1900	9d purple and blue	7·00	3·00	15·00	6·00
211	1887–1900	1s green	20·00	3·50	70·00	10·00
235	1887–1900	4d green and brown	8·00	1·00	22·00	3·00
294	1887–1900	5d purple and blue	3·00	1·75	7·00	2·00
298	1887–1900	6d purple	2·50	1·00	5·00	1·75
311	1887–1900	10d purple and red	6·00	3·50	14·00	6·00
314	1887–1900	1s green and red	4·50	1·25	7·00	2·00
316	1887–1900	2/6d lilac	28·00	8·00	80·00	14·00
318	1887–1900	5s red	35·00	9·00	110·00	18·00
319	1887–1900	10s blue	65·00	28·00	200·00	55·00

SG Cat. No.	Date	Stamp	1975 Unused	Used	1977 Unused	Used
			£	£	£	£
320	1887–1900	£1 green	165·00	45·00	425·00	90·00
325	1911–12	½d green	0·40	0·08	1·25	0·30
329	1911–12	1d red	0·40	0·08	0·80	0·25
334	1912	½d green	3·00	1·50	6·00	3·50
336	1912	1d red	2·50	1·50	5·00	3·50
362	1912–22	1½d brown	0·05	0·05	0·10	0·10
381	1912–22	5d brown	1·25	0·50	2·75	1·75
387	1912–22	7d olive-green	3·50	1·00	7·00	2·25
390	1912–22	8d black on yellow	7·00	1·75	16·00	4·50
392	1912–22	9d black	3·00	0·80	4·00	1·50
393a	1912–22	9d olive-green	20·00	2·25	45·00	10·00
394	1912–22	10d blue	4·00	1·50	7·00	6·00
395	1912–22	1s brown	2·50	0·25	5·00	50·00
397	1913	½d green	20·00	10·00	45·00	25·00
398	1913	1d red	35·00	18·00	85·00	50·00
414	1913–18	2/6d brown	18·00	4·00	40·00	8·00
416	1913–18	5s red	20·00	5·00	45·00	11·00
417	1913–18	10s blue	40·00	10·00	85·00	25·00
428	1924–26	10d blue	4·50	1·25	15·00	6·00
430	1924	1d red	6·00	6·00	6·00	6·00
431	1924	1½d brown	8·00	8·00	10·00	10·00
432	1925	1d red	10·00	8·00	10·00	10·00
433	1925	1½d brown	30·00	25·00	35·00	30·00
438	1929	£1 black	190·00	110·00	400·00	250·00
448	1934–36	10d blue	3·00	0·50	10·00	3·00
449	1934–36	1s brown	3·50	0·25	18·00	0·40
450	1934	2/6d brown	15·00	1·75	40·00	2·00

No.	Year	Description				
451	1934	5s red	3·50	28·00	70·00	5·00
452	1934	10s blue	5·00	40·00	100·00	12·00
456	1935	2½d blue	3·00	5·00	4·75	4·00
474a	1937–47	1½d plum	0·35	1·75	2·50	0·50
476	1939–48	2/6d brown	1·25	7·00	22·00	4·00
476a	1939–48	2/6d green	0·20	3·50	6·00	0·30
477	1939–48	5s red	0·50	7·50	15·00	0·70
478	1939–48	10s dark blue	5·00	50·00	100·00	8·00
478a	1939–48	10s bright blue	75·00	12·00	12·00	1·00
478b	1939–48	£1 brown	5·00	7·00	12·00	10·00
484	1940	3d violet	2·50	3·00	4·00	3·50
494	1948	£1 blue	25·00	20·00	20·00	20·00
512	1951	£1 brown	4·00	10·00	25·00	6·00
524	1952	7d green	0·40	1·00	3·00	0·75
526	1952	9d bronze-green	0·40	4·50	12·00	0·50
527	1952	10d blue	0·40	4·50	11·00	1·25
528	1952	11d plum	2·00	9·00	20·00	4·50
529	1952	1s bistre	0·12	1·50	0·75	0·12
531	1952	1/6d indigo	0·30	4·50	18·00	0·40
538	1955–58	10s blue	2·50	25·00	35·00	5·00
539	1955–58	£1 black	3·00	45·00	85·00	5·00
549	1955–58	7d green	0·75	16·00	30·00	1·00
551	1955–58	9d bronze-green	0·35	10·00	15·00	0·40
554	1955–58	1s bistre	0·12	8·00	12·00	0·12
555	1955–58	1/3d green	0·30	10·00	18·00	0·35
556	1955–58	1/6d indigo	0·35	10·00	22·00	0·40
558	1957	4d blue	0·50	1·00	1·50	0·75
559	1957	1/3d green	6·00	4·50	5·50	7·50
565	1957	2½d red	2·50	2·50	6·00	4·00

SG Cat. No.	Date	Stamp	1975 Unused £	1975 Used £	1977 Unused £	1977 Used £
589	1958–61	1½d green	25·00	12·00	45·00	30·00
591	1958–61	2½d red	6·00	3·00	10·00	8·00
597a	1959–63	10s blue	2·50	0·60	5·00	0·60
606	1959	2½d red	5·50	5·50	9·00	7·50
607	1959	3d lilac	7·00	5·50	12·00	6·00
609	1959	4½d blue	22·00	18·00	40·00	25·00
625	1961	1/6d red and blue	1·25	1·25	2·50	2·50
630	1961	1/3d green and blue	1·75	1·75	3·00	3·00
641	1963	1/6d sepia, yellow and blue	1·75	1·75	3·00	2·25
645	1963	1/6d blue and black	1·50	1·75	2·25	2·25
650	1964	2/6d deep slate-purple	2·00	2·00	3·00	2·50
677	1965	9d black, violet, orange and maroon	2·00	1·00	3·00	3·00
678	1965	1/3d green, black and blue	2·00	1·50	3·00	3·00
712	1966	1/3d multicoloured	0·20	0·25	0·60	0·50
762	1967–68	£1 black	5·50	1·00	6·00	2·50
789	1969	10s ultramarine	18·00	2·00	11·00	10·00
790	1969	£1 black	3·50	0·75	2·00	1·50
829	1970	10p cerise	0·50	0·20	1·75	0·20
889	1971	9p multicoloured	0·85	0·95	1·25	1·25
900	1972	9p multicoloured	0·85	0·85	1·25	1·25
907	1972	7½p multicoloured	0·75	0·75	1·00	1·00
917	1972	20p slate-purple, reddish violet and silver	0·90	0·50	1·00	1·00
942	1973	20p brown and silver	0·70	0·45	1·00	1·00
953	1974	10p multicoloured	0·40	0·40	0·50	0·50

8 FORGERIES, ERRORS AND OTHERS

Some forgeries are worth more than the genuine stamp, just as flaws and errors can increase the value of a stamp many times over. Both can evoke the same excited enthusiasm from the collector/investor. The right kind of find can be worth a lot of money.

Propaganda forgery

Propaganda forgeries are becoming more and more popular. One of these is the propaganda issue produced by Great Britain and the United States during the last war, showing Hitler as a skull-like demon. This is now fetching good money, whereas not so long ago it was difficult to give it away for nothing.

Fakes

One thing the collector/investor must watch for is the fake. A popular trick is for someone to try to sell a so-called mint stamp when it is only a re-gummed one. The expert will be able to detect the re-gummed stamp at once, so get advice if you feel that there is something wrong. Don't get directly involved until you are expert enough yourself to be able to see and feel the difference between a genuine mint stamp and a re-gummed fake.

Genuine stamps are sometimes altered to increase their value, and steps you should take when trying to verify a possible fake include the following:

    (a) Check the cancellation mark.

    (b) Check to see if any perforation holes have been covered up by someone smoothing over the stamp reverse with fresh gum.

    (c) Look to see if anything has been rubbed out on the stamp.

    (d) Check to see if the stamp has been retouched in any way.

    (e) Check the back of the stamp to see if there are any irregularities.

(f) Check the edges for repaired tears.

(g) Check that no perforation teeth have been surreptitiously stuck on.

(h) Check each corner carefully to see if any have been repaired.

To make a profit, the people involved in faking will get up to anything. Here is a check list: printing flaws; mirror images; graphite line; phosphor bands; changing colours; plate numbers; watermarks. You name it and it has been faked at one time or another, so beware!

French forgery

The 10c 'Sower' stamp is very popular with French specialists. This stamp was forged in great quantities about seventy years ago, but today the forgery is worth a lot more than the genuine early twentieth century 10c stamp issued at around the same time. There are plenty of the genuine stamps on the market.

The British 1s stamp 1872

About the only time the Post Office in this country was hoodwinked was when someone at the London Stock Exchange, between June 1872 and July 1873, supplied forged 1s (one shilling) stamps to brokers for the payment of telegrams. This was not discovered until many years after the incident. A noted stamp dealer, Charles Nissen, came upon some old telegram forms and pronounced the stamps to be forgeries. There was a full investigation and it was found that the forger had died some years earlier. The stamps live on, however, and these forgeries are worth more than the genuine article.

The German forger

George Fouré was the editor of *Berliner Briefmarken Zeitung*, a German stamp journal. In this publication, he attacked all stamp forgers and forgeries, while manufacturing his own counterfeits. He had access to plates and dyes and purported to borrow them for study purposes. Because he was an accredited expert philatelist he aroused no suspicions. Like most forgers, he then went too far. Everyone had been amazed at all the rare stamps he had been 'discovering', but when he produced German covers with unknown postmarks, the game was up. Tests proved that the dyes used were aniline; during the alleged period of issue, however, only vegetable dyes were in existence. Fouré vanished, but his expert forgeries still cause problems in the philatelic world in Germany.

The international forger

One of the most famous forgers of all time was Jean de Sperati. This designer and artist was so good at his work that he even fooled some of the expert philatelic committee members authorized by the Philatelic Society to value stamps. He had an international organization which operated from printing works in France, Italy and Switzerland. Some of his forgeries fetched very high prices, because they were accepted as genuine rare stamps, after the expert committees had underwritten them with their own guarantee. They believed completely that the stamps were the real thing. Sperati was later sentenced to a year in prison for fraud and forgery. When he came out, he put his collection up for sale. This became known as the Sperati Collection, and he sold his stamps quite legally under the title of Philatelic Art. Dealers purchased various sets, and it has been said that some of his forgeries of rare stamps were sold for very high prices on the commercial market.

He forged stamps with various face values, and countries and dates to look out for include the following:

Greece	1861
Hungary	1871
Sweden	1855
France	1850
Uruguay	1856

He also reproduced rare stamps of Switzerland and Hawaii, and early British and British Empire stamps, including Ceylon, the Gold Coast, Lagos, Mauritius, Newfoundland, Malta and Hong Kong. In the mid 1950s, by which time the master forger was an old man with failing eyesight, the British Philatelic Association managed to get the balance of his forgeries. The Association had them all specially marked so that they could never again be sold as the real thing.

Dealer guarantees

Collector/investors who deal through reputable dealers, those who give guarantees, have nothing to fear. Such dealers have expert knowledge, and know every trick in the book. They cannot afford to have their reputations damaged, so they take pains to ensure that everything is as it should be. They can be particularly helpful over the old albums that sometimes come up for sale which may hold hidden snares. These probably contain some genuine old stamps, but there may also be worthless fakes (stamps that have been doctored) of which even the album owner is unaware. They could, on the other hand, contain valuable forgeries and genuine rarities. Once you have gained experience, it will be exciting to find out what these old collections contain. In the meantime stay with your dealer's guarantees.

Errors and flaws

Mistakes made by engravers or designers are known as errors, whereas those caused during printing are officially known as flaws. The error can be in the inscription, colour, surcharge paper, watermark, etc. These deviations or variations come under the general heading of varieties. However, if an error in the basic design has been brought forward by the engraver without being spotted during the entire issue of the stamps – and the entire issue contains this error – it is not classed as a variety. The term variety is used in philately only when a small fraction of a given issue has been released containing the error.

All the facts of any particular stamp with an error should be fully evaluated before any investment is contemplated.

The expert philatelist, whether or not he is looking for errors, today depends more and more on scientific equipment. This usually consists of an ultra-violet lamp and a spectrometer. The former detects, among other things, alterations and repairs, and the latter helps to analyse ink, gum and exact colour. It would be possible to find, with close enough inspection, that every stamp differs in some infinitesimal way from every other in the same issue. Thankfully, the errors which make a stamp a variety can be established under the inspection of normal sight and touch. The most famous British variety is the 1½d stamp issued between 1918 and 1921. On certain printings every stamp at the right-hand end of the row had the inscription THREE HALFPENCF – an 'F' instead of an 'E'. When this error was corrected, the F became an E with a long stroke and a prominent serif. In this case, the corrected error, which is slightly harder to detect with the human eye, is far more valuable than the original error, which is both readily available and easy to spot. Another famous British error was the 2½d 1935 Silver Jubilee Stamp. Three sheets printed in Prussian blue (instead of the official ultramarine blue) got into circulation via a London post office. An observant collector happened to be in the right place at the right time, and he bought more than 300 of the 360 stamps issued.

Some stamps with errors or flaws are not valuable, as in the following case: back in 1962 stamp investors who had obtained the U.S. Dag Hammerskjold four-cent commemorative stamp, thought they had made a real coup. During the printing, some of the stamps had acquired an inverted plate number, together with a horizontal area of white around the United Nations building. About four hundred containing these errors came on to the market, and their price soared to about $5,000 each. Unfortunately, as soon as the price started climbing, the U.S. Postmaster General showed his displeasure at all the profit being made by promptly issuing large numbers of the stamps with the same flaws. He caused a few people to lose a lot of money.

9 AIRMAIL STAMPS

Aerophilately can be a fascinating way of tracing the development of aeronautics. Prior to 1859 there had been several balloon flights, but there is no record of any mail being carried by those early pioneers. However, in August 1859 an American named John Wise set off in his balloon, *Jupiter* from the town of Lafayette in the state of Indiana, with a consignment of mail. It is interesting to note that when the notice of this flight was printed in the local paper, no specific destination was given. This is because it was not possible to navigate the balloon. John Wise had a theory that the upper atmospheric winds blew towards the east, and he therefore invited members of the public to have their letters 'to friends in the East' carried by balloon.

The letters, all prepaid, were collected and endorsed by the local postmaster. The normal address was written on each envelope, plus the words, 'Via Balloon Jupiter', and the arrangement was that wherever the balloon descended, John Wise would post the mail at the nearest post office, from which it would be sent on in the normal way.

Although *Jupiter* managed to reach a fair altitude, there was no trace of wind at all and the balloon merely drifted. Five hours or so later, Wise and *Jupiter* hit the ground in the town of Crawfordsville, just thirty miles south of Lafayette, and from there, the mail was duly delivered. To mark the centenary of this flight, a seven-cent airmail stamp was issued in the United States showing *Jupiter*.

The first government-sponsored airmail

In 1870, France was beaten by Germany in the Franco–Prussian war, and Paris was held under a siege which lasted four months. It was essential to keep lines of communication open with the outside world, and several methods for carrying mail were tried. One was to enclose the letters in metal containers which were floated down the river Seine in the hope that they would pass the Prussian ranks. Another was to send them in free-flight balloons, i.e. those that carried only articles and no people. However, these attempts were mostly unsuccessful, and the balloons and metal containers were destroyed by the Germans. It was not until the French employed man-carrying balloons that they were able to get letters out of Paris.

Several man-carrying balloons were already in existence during the siege. These included the *Ville de Florence*, the *Napoléon*, the *Hirondelle*, the *Céleste* and the *Neptune*, the last of which made a flight on 23 September, carrying a sizeable amount of mail. It was piloted by its owner, Jules Duruof, who reached Craconville (near Evreux) safely, and from there despatched the mail.

The success of the *Neptune* encouraged the authorities to set up workshops for the making of new balloons and in all, sixty-five were built. These carried the first government-sponsored airmails, and were soon operating a regular service out of Paris, manned by marines, professional pilots and some volunteers. It was an efficiently run project and became a source of employment for hundreds of Parisians, some of whom had been rendered redundant by the siege. Out of the sixty-five balloons the incredibly high number of fifty-seven reached their destinations safely.

The rate for letters was set at twenty centimes, which had to be paid in advance, and the weight was restricted to a maximum of four grams. Because the amount of mail to be ballooned out of Paris steadily increased, the authorities reinstated unmanned balloons to help cope with the demand. The rate for this unmanned service was only ten centimes, and a new aircard was introduced which weighed three grams.

It was during the siege of Paris that the first airmail postmark was introduced. This was in the form of a hand-stamp which was applied to the reverse of letters to be despatched by balloon. It was also used as the official *cachet* on the correspondence of a company – 'The Company of Military Balloonists' – which was formed by three of the balloon pioneers, Nadar, Dartois and Duruof. The red *cachet*, which was round in shape, had the words REPUBLIQUE – FRANÇAISE round the outer edge, and in the centre, arranged in four lines, were the words AEROSTIERS. NADAR. DARTOIS. DURUOF. These postmarks are very much sought after and can fetch high prices on the collectors' market.

Balloons and airships

Ballooning was a very popular hobby in Britain during the nineteenth century, and although it was still not possible to steer or navigate the balloons to a definite destination, many balloonists carried postcards which they dropped at random. Each card usually had a message written on it asking the finder to post it back to the balloonist giving details of where it was found. In this way it was possible to trace the course of these early flights.

On 6 October 1870 an unmanned balloon was released from Crystal Palace carrying a batch of mail which was postmarked HYTHE. The balloon came down on a farm near Folkestone in Kent, and from there the mail was forwarded by the more conventional method. All the letters reached their destinations, and although this flight was a one-off novelty, the postcards carried on that occasion were in fact the first British airmails, and are keenly sought after by airmail enthusiasts.

There were many other balloon flights in the latter half of the nineteenth century, mostly in conjunction with special occasions such as festivals, national holidays, etc. These took place not only in Britain, but also in other parts of Europe, particularly in France, Germany and Italy. The coronation of Edward VII saw increased ballooning activity in Britain and by this time, balloons were becoming more and more sophisticated. Some were constructed so that a supply of gas could be kept on board, thus allowing the balloon to stay in the air for long periods, sometimes for days and even weeks. One of the most famous long-distance flights was sponsored by the newspaper *The Daily Herald*, and was made by a man named Caudron in a giant balloon called *Mammoth*. This balloon, a marvellous piece of workmanship, was built in two tiers, like a double-decker. On 12 October 1907, it set off from Crystal Palace, and the next evening it came down in Sweden, having crossed the North Sea at a height of 12,000 feet. A batch of mail was carried on the flight, in the form of souvenir postcards. Caudron posted most of these in the Swedish village of Tosse. Some cards, however, were dropped out of the balloon a short time before the descent, and these were found and posted from Mellerud. All of the *Mammoth* cards are highly prized today, in particular those which were sent from Mellerud. It is interesting to note that these cards had not been prepaid, as was the usual procedure for balloon post. Instead, the sum of twopence had to be paid by each person to whom the cards were addressed. If you are lucky enough to obtain one of these cards, you can be confident that you have a very good investment.

Between balloons and aeroplanes came an intermediate, the dirigible balloon. This represented a great leap forward in aeronautics. The dirigible's most important feature was an internal combustion engine which made it possible, for the first time, to navigate. Among people associated with the development of such airships were the Lebaudy brothers from France, Alberto Santos Dumont from Brazil, and, the most celebrated of all, Count Ferdinand Von Zeppelin from Germany, who was responsible for the famous Zeppelin airships. His first airship flew over Lake Constance in 1900. The following year many giant Zeppelins were constructed which carried many passengers, and postcards were usually thrown overboard during the flights. These cards were specially designed and carried such messages as 'Greetings on Board the Zeppelin Airship', and details of the flight including altitude, weather conditions, etc. Most of the cards thrown from Zeppelins bore *cachets* in red, grey, or violet, giving instructions to the finder to post the card at their nearest post office, and requesting him to give some details on the card regarding weather conditions at the time of finding it. To ensure that the cards were not blown about too much after they were thrown overboard, small weights were often attached to them by short cords. The names of some of the Zeppelin airships were *Hansa*, *Victoria Luise*, *Sachsen*, and *Schwaben*.

In 1913 the first official airmail stamps were issued, costing twenty-five pfennigs. The cards were carried by the Zeppelins, which by now were developed to such a high degree that they could make long leisure trips. Official postmarks had been introduced the previous year for the occasion of the Aviation Festival at Hesse, when there was also a special issue of stamps in denominations of 10pf, 20pf, and 30pf. These were for use only during the two weeks of the Hesse festival.

Plans for an Anglo-German Airship Expedition were drawn up in 1913, but World War One put an end to that idea. It is interesting to note that special stamps were issued in order to help raise money for the projected expedition.

These came in two denominations, twenty-five pfennig and one mark, and they showed the flags of Germany and Britain with the airship. The twenty-five pfennig stamp was blue and the one mark stamp was multicoloured. Both are extremely rare.

Aeroplanes

Although there had been numerous previous attempts to construct and fly aeroplanes, it was not until December 1903 that the first successful flight was made by the American Wright brothers in their biplane, in North Carolina. Much progress has been made since, and it is interesting to see the way in which things have progressed from the first frail bone-shaker of the Wright brothers. Various types of small privately owned aeroplanes were introduced; then came the big commercial airliners, jets, jumbo jets and the magnificent Concorde.

Every advance in aeronautics has been marked by special stamps. These include various American issues featuring the Wright brothers in 1928, 1949 and 1953. The celebrated brothers have also been shown on stamps of other countries, as were many of the other early pioneers such as Ernest Archdeacon, the Bonnet-Labranche brothers and Henri Jarman. The machines were also featured on many stamps. These had names such as *June Bug*, *Jenny*, and *Gelber-Hund*. Several postmarks were issued to mark important aeronautic events. One interesting example featured the different points of take-off for the famous Monte Carlo air rally of 1914. These were London, Paris, Brussels, Madrid, Milan, Gotha and Vienna.

Before 1911 mail had been carried by balloons, airships and aeroplanes, but there had been no official flight organized exclusively for transporting mail. The postcards that had been carried were mostly of a commemorative nature, except in emergency circumstances such as during the siege of Paris. In February 1911, however, an exhibition was held in India – the United Provinces Industrial and Agricultural Exhibition – and the Postmaster General of the United Provinces, in association with Sir Walter Wyndham, at that time known as Captain Wyndham, authorized a Frenchman by the name of Pequet to make a five-mile flight carrying well over 6,000 pieces of mail from the exhibition ground at Allahabad, to Naine Junction. The postmark on the letters and postcards read 'First Aerial Post – VP Exhibition Allahabad.' In the centre of the postmark there was a picture of the Humber-Sommer biplane in flight over the mountains. Several postcards were produced as commemoratives, and in 1961 a set of stamps was issued by the Indian Government to mark the fiftieth anniversary of this first airmail flight. These stamps show the original postmark, as well as a Boeing 707 jet.

The same Captain Wyndham was responsible for organizing the British Aerial post between London and Windsor, as part of the coronation celebrations for George V. Postcards were issued for this occasion which cost sixpence halfpenny, and envelopes which cost one shilling and sixpence. Both the cards and the envelopes had stamps already on them, so there was no extra change for postage. The postmark read either 'From London to Windsor', or 'From Windsor to London'. Perhaps the most interesting aspect of the coronation airmail was the part played by colour. The cards and envelopes used by official personnel were violet in colour. Other people used cards of red, green, mustard and brown.

After the London–Windsor project there were no further official British airmail flights until World War One, although there had been several privately organized airmail flights in different parts of the country. In 1915, however, the government was forced to use aeroplanes in order to send official and military mail between England and Belgium. The route, via Folkestone, became known as the King Albert Line. The government also used aeroplanes during the war to distribute propaganda literature and a variety of civil-service leaflets which advertised loans and benefits available to the public.

Commercial airlines

After World War One, a great many small British aircraft companies were formed to cater for the surge of interest in flying. The forerunners of today's mighty aviation organizations, they were not without their problems. Although there was a great demand for short joy rides and novelty trips, there wasn't enough regular trade to keep the smaller companies in business, and many went bankrupt. A few, such as Daimler Airways, Instone Air Lines and Handley Page Transport, managed to keep going, but business was slow and the prospects of survival were poor. The problem was solved by amalgamation in 1924, when these three companies teamed up with British Marine Air Navigation to form Imperial Airways Ltd.

Progress was good, and in a matter of months business had increased to such a level that many European flights which had operated only at weekends were put on a daily schedule. Within two years, Imperial Airways Ltd was operating long-distance flights to Baghdad, the Persian Gulf and India, and the company was made responsible for carrying airmail to Cairo and Baghdad, previously the task of the Royal Air Force. This mail flight was made every two weeks, and postage cost one shilling per ounce. In 1929 the airmail service was extended to Karachi, and the stops along the way – Athens, Alexandria, Gaza, and Basra – were also served. Souvenir envelopes were issued by Imperial Airways to mark this occasion and the postage rates were divided into two categories. The rate for mail going to Egypt and Palestine was twopence halfpenny per half ounce, and the rate for India and the ports along the Persian Gulf, was sixpence per half ounce. By 1937 the company was also carrying mail to Australia, America, Africa, the Far East and the Middle East.

In 1940 Imperial Airways amalgamated with the smaller British Airways to form British Overseas Airways Corporation (BOAC). After World War II a new commercial company, British European Airways (BEA), was formed. It was decided that BEA should operate all internal and European flights and that BOAC should fly the intercontinental flights, except for the South Atlantic route which was being flown by British South American Airways. Eventually this company amalgamated with BOAC. In 1964 the South Atlantic route was operated by an independent airline, British United Airways (BUA), which, in 1970, amalgamated with the Scottish company, Caledonian Airways, to form British Caledonian Airways. The new company continued to operate the South Atlantic route. By this time jet propelled airliners were in general use.

In other countries airmail also developed rapidly, and a gigantic system of worldwide routes developed, so that mail can now be delivered by air to any part of the globe.

10 ACCESSORIES

If you intend to make a profit from your stamps, you must present them in such a way as to impress potential customers. To do this, it will be necessary to obtain the best equipment you can afford. There are several essential basic requirements: an album, hinges, tweezers, catalogues, sweat boxes and a duplicate book. In addition, you will find these accessories helpful: a magnifying glass, a watermark detector, a colour guide, a direct-measurement scale, a perforation gauge, gummed labels and arrows.

Albums

A vast selection of albums is available in all shapes and sizes. These fall into two main types, the fast-bound printed album which has spaces allocated for stamps, and the loose-leaf type. The latter offers far greater scope for your personal arrangement. You will find it helpful to choose a good quality paper with a light quadrillé ground, as this will assist you to centre the stamps properly when you mount them. Some albums have black pages which contrast effectively with the colours of the stamps. Some pages have double-hinged edges which allow the page to lie flat when it is opened; but these are a trifle more expensive than ordinary rigid leaves.

Perhaps the most important aspect of your album is the mechanism which holds the pages together. There are several types available, some rather complicated; the best is the multi-ringed binder which, like the linen double-hinged leaves, allows the pages to lie flat when opened. Make sure that you insert protective sheets between the pages of stamps. You can buy sheets of transparent paper from your dealer for this purpose. Don't overlook this, because you might often come across stamps that have been postmarked with a particular type of ink which rubs off easily. If there are no interleaving sheets, then the ink will mark the reverse of the previous page.

When you have chosen your album, take care that you

don't cram too many pages into it. This will only result in breaking the grasping mechanism. It is much better to present your stamps in two or three well arranged volumes than in one bulging book which looks as if it is about to explode. It is best to stand your album up on a shelf when storing it, unless you have a special case or storage box. Take care to give the stamps plenty of fresh air. Leave the pages exposed from time to time, and make certain that you store your stamps in a dry atmosphere, especially if the pages are black. If you become suspicious of any trace of dampness or discolouration, do not take any chances, but re-mount your stamps immediately.

Hinges

In order to mount your stamps, you will require hinges. These are small gummed pieces of thin paper which are inexpensive to buy and which are essential to do the job properly. Unlike glue, which dries hard and fast, the gum with which the hinges are coated peels off easily from both the page of the album and the stamp. If this peeling is done carefully, there should be no damage whatsoever to the stamp, and no unsightly smudge left on the page. This is because the hinge has a double layer of gum.

Tweezers

You should always use tweezers when moving expensive stamps. The reason is that the moisture left by the hands on the surface does, after some time, have a damaging effect. So, in order to be well rehearsed for your expensive stamps, you might as well get into the habit of using tweezers early on with your common stamps. With a little practice you will find that the tweezers can be easily manipulated. They should be used not only for mounting your stamps, but also for preparing them, i.e. floating or placing them in sweat boxes, and for turning mounted stamps over in order to inspect the reverse sides. In fact the tweezers should eventually become, as it were, an extension of your own fingers, and should be used each time you touch the stamps.

There are several types of tweezers on the market, some with pointed prongs, some spade shaped, some with round ends. Your choice is entirely a matter of preference, but

An unused strip of twelve Penny Blacks which was sold for £6,500 in 1973.

Above: The 1849 Bermuda Penny 'Perot' sold for £30,000 at Stanley Gibbons's auction in April 1977 of part of the fabulous Claude Cartier collection.

Below: Out of reach of most investors, probably the world's most valuable stamp: the British Guiana One Cent Black on Magenta of 1856, at present valued by Stanley Gibbons in their famous Stamps of the World stamp catalogue at £300,000. This price also makes it probably the most valuable single item in the world in terms of size and substance.

Above: An unused example of Great Britain's rare 1867–83 £1 stamp printed from plate 1 – which realized £4,750 in auction in 1976.

Below: A superb used example of Canada's 12d black on laid paper, sold for £19,000 at auction in London in September 1977.

An item of historical and local interest – a set of the German
occupation 'Swastika'-overprinted stamps of Jersey – now worth at
least £2,000.

Early airmail: a very rare entire letter flown out of Paris by balloon on 26 January 1871 during the Siege of Paris – it realized £280 at auction in 1976.

A superb unused block of twelve of Great Britain's 1841
imperforate Penny Red, with original gum. This item has
appreciated in value as follows:

1962	£90	1974	£400
1968	£100	1975	£700
1972	£225	1976/7	£1,100
1973	£300	1978/9	?

Above: A historical curiosity and a valuable investment: this envelope was sent from Margate on 30 July 1876 to one John S. Hiley, in service with General Custer in the Bighorn Expedition. The envelope was returned to the sender explaining that 'John S. Hiley was killed on Little Bighorn Mountain on June 25, 1876'.

Below: A rare airmail envelope bearing an example of the famous Newfoundland 'Hawker' stamp.

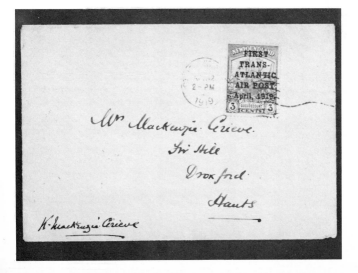

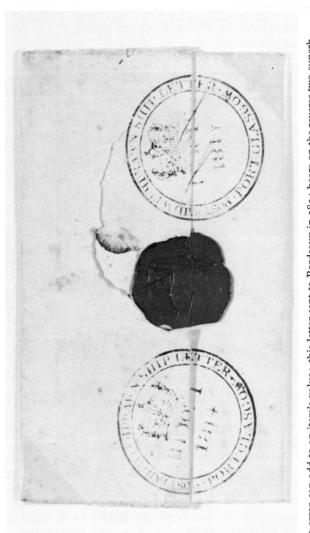

An error can add to an item's value: this letter sent to Bordeaux in 1814 bears on the reverse two superb strikes of the circular POST PAID WITHDRAWN SHIP LETTER PORT GLASGOW/CROWN/DATE stamp. In one strike the date is inverted; presumably the authorities noticed the error as the date is deleted in manuscript. A second, correct, strike was then applied.

under no circumstances must you use eyebrow tweezers or any other type with sharp ends. It is important that the tweezers leave no mark where they come in contact with your stamps, so it is wise to test with a small piece of paper before buying. If there is any mark where the tweezers touch the paper, then they are too sharp to be trusted with your stamps. Remember, too, to be sure that the tweezers are rust-proof.

Catalogues

You will need a range of current catalogues to keep you informed on the prevailing market values. These list the stamps from the various countries and give the current price for each stamp. New issues appear from time to time, and it is advisable to keep your catalogues up to date. Catalogues normally include wide selections of illustrations which serve as good guides for identifying your stamps. The listings show you the different dates of issue, and this, again, is a great help when you arrange your stamps.

Probably the best catalogues to buy are those published by Stanley Gibbons, because it is the numbers used in these which are generally referred to at fairs and auctions in this country. Gibbons also publish an advanced catalogue which goes into great detail and is extremely useful to anyone with a specialist or thematic collection. Other countries have their own catalogues. Scott's *Standard Postage Stamp Catalogue* is popular in the United States.

Sweat boxes

These are used for separating used stamps from their envelopes, and can be bought in philately shops. They act in much the same way as the pads of damp blotting paper described in the chapter entitled 'How to Arrange your Collection'. The moisture is absorbed by the envelope, thus making it possible to remove the stamp without too much trouble.

Duplicate book

You will need a duplicate book in which to keep not only duplicate stamps, but also stamps awaiting mounting. This can be any type of book, preferably with a firm hand-book binding, which will protect the stamps. Enter some transparent strips between the pages and place the stamps in the small pockets. If you do not wish to keep the loose premounted stamps in the same book as your duplicates, you can keep them safely in strong transparent envelopes. Some people like to keep a list of stamps they are looking for, and the back pages of your duplicate book can be useful for this purpose. As you obtain each stamp, you draw a neat line through the entry so as to keep your list up to date.

Magnifying glass

A magnifying glass will enable you to distinguish small details on your stamps without endangering your eyesight. It is not necessary to get an extra strong glass, just one which will enlarge the details sufficiently for you to read them with ease. Your glass should have some sort of protective cover, because if it gets scratched it may refract light, thus making it difficult to read the details without their appearing to be distorted. There are many good magnifiers on the market which are illuminated by means of batteries; these are very helpful in making a thorough inspection of the stamps.

Watermark detector

This is a small tray which has a black bottom; it is used in conjunction with benzine to bring up the watermark on the reverse of a stamp. The stamp is laid face downward on the detector slab, or tray, and a tiny amount of benzine is poured on the stamp. This should bring up the watermark for a short time, but you must watch carefully, because as soon as the benzine evaporates the watermark will disappear. You can buy benzine in small bottles fitted with drop dispensers, which makes it possible to measure out one drop at a time. This guards against the danger of flooding the stamp. However, most stamps, except those of the photogravure type, can take a fair amount of benzine without any detrimental effects.

There are some fairly advanced watermark detectors on the market which work by means of ultra-violet rays. They show up not only the watermark, but also any irregularities that may exist. These detectors are more expensive than the ordinary kind, but since they are so versatile, you may feel justified in spending the extra money.

Perforation gauge

It is important to be able to establish accurately the number of perforations on any given stamp; this could mean a big difference in the price you realize. Some stamps, issued in the same design as others, might be taken for duplicates by the untrained eye. But there might be a big difference in their value, depending upon the number of perforations. There is a universally accepted gauge for determining stamp perforations, which is standardized according to a measurement of two centimetres. This gauge is a small card, marked out in much the same way as an ordinary ruler, and sectioned off in lengths of two centimetres. Each section contains a row of dots which vary in number from those in every other section. A gauge number is printed beside each section which tells you the number of dots in the section.

In order to gauge the perforations on your stamp, simply place it next to the card and move it along until the perforation marks on your stamp coincide exactly with the dots in any one of the sections. If you have a stamp with, say, thirteen perforations, it will exactly match the section marked 13 on the card. You would refer to that stamp as Perf. 13.

Some stamps, however, have an unequal number of perforations. These are called compound perforations. To measure the gauge of such stamps, you must check all four sides. The catalogue should give you a guide as to the number of perforations for which to look. When referring to these compounds, you should state the top and bottom measurement first, then the right- and left-hand sides. For example, if the top and bottom measure eleven perforations to every two centimetres, and the two sides measure twelve perforations, this would be referred to as Perf. 11×12. Remember that compounds come in a variety of combinations. Some have an equal number of perforations on the top and bottom, and a different equal number on the two sides. Others can have three sides measuring the same, with the fourth different. In some cases all four sides of the stamp may each have a different number of perforations. These are referred to in a clockwise manner: the top row first; the right-hand side second, the bottom third, and the left-hand side fourth. To recap, therefore, the perforation references would be as follows:

(A) All four sides the same   Perf. 15
(B) Two opposite sides equal   Perf. 14 × 15
(C) One side different   Perf. 14 × 15 × 14 × 14
(D) All four sides different   Perf. 14 × 15 × 13 × 12

Sometimes gauges change as the long row of perforations continues down a sheet of stamps. They may start off by giving a regular measurement of, say, twelve perforations. Then gradually this number will increase to, say, twelve and one-half or thirteen. This irregularity is caused by the pins being wrongly placed in the perforating machine, and the measurement would be referred to as 14 to 15. This term should not be confused with another which is used to denote that the measurement contains a fraction (other than a half). For instance, if the gauge reading were between $14\frac{1}{2}$ and 15 you could refer to it as $14\frac{3}{4}$ or $14\frac{1}{2}$,15. To calculate fractions, take into consideration that a unit consists of the area of an entire perforation hole, plus half of each of the perforation teeth at either side of the hole; the other halves of course belong to the following perforations. If the measurement falls between two teeth, exactly in the centre of a perforation hole, this would count as a half, and so on.

There is a gauge available called the 'Instanta' which gives fractional and decimal readings. This is proving immensely popular as it makes precise readings possible.

Colour guide

Because the colours used in philately are peculiar to the hobby, it is advisable to buy a colour guide. You may think you know the difference between the various shades of, say, blue or green, but it is well to be certain. You may be surprised to find that some of the shades differ slightly from your usual conception of that particular colour. The colour guide gives all the main colours in which stamps are issued universally. There are 100 different colours in all, and when you bear in mind that the surrounding details of a stamp can be a misleading factor in establishing the main colour, then the guide is well worth having.

Gummed labels

To help present your stamps neatly you may wish to purchase gummed labels which are specially made for philatelists. These come in various shapes and sizes and have all the necessary terms printed on them, dates, colours, type, letters etc. You can also buy little gummed paper arrows, as described in Chapter Four. It is also possible to buy transfers containing all the necessary terms, which can easily be rubbed on to the pages of your album.

11 BUSINESS GUIDELINES

Before setting up in business as a stamp dealer, ask yourself if you have gained enough knowledge to safeguard your customers, your own reputation and your capital. It is most important to know exactly what you are doing – mistakes can prove very costly. It takes years to gain the knowledge necessary to set up as a general dealer; however, some people specialize in a certain type or variety of stamp. This of course has its obvious limitations, but the advantage is that you would not have to spend as many years studying as you would have to if you were covering the whole field.

Many of today's dealers learnt their trade by first working for an established firm. Many of them have remained one-man-businesses. Behind the big press advertising campaigns they have small operations, because that is where their profitability lies. The successful dealers have learnt their trade by extensive study of the market, by practical involvement and by constant handling of stamps. You can't have too much experience; too little could cause your business to go under.

Many mail order dealers working on a part-time basis have the best of both worlds. They have an income from a regular job, and the low operating costs of working from home. The full-time stamp dealer has to have large capital resources both in financial backing and in good quality stock, not just common everyday stamps that everyone has got already. He must have the business acumen to be able to maximize his turnover, and more importantly, his profit margins. His costs must be kept to an absolute basic minimum, with all advertising expenditure properly worked out so that returns show a consistent profit. His judgment must be impeccable – buying for next-to-nothing today, and selling at good prices in the future. By using experience, knowledge, keen judgment, and that elusive sixth sense, it is possible to be a successful stamp dealer. Some have done it in the past, and others will succeed in the future.

Stamps on approval

Stamps are normally sent out on 7 days approval to customers: (a) known to the dealer; (b) against prior cash payment; (c) when satisfactory references have been supplied.

Buying through the post

It is a good idea to instruct all would-be clients to deliver stamps to you for your valuation and offer. A simple instruction in all press advertising could read something like this:

> Send all quality material to us by registered post. We will write by return stating how much we are prepared to pay. On receiving your reply we either send our cheque for settlement, or, if you have refused our offer, return your stamps. We guarantee prompt payment. Will all overseas sellers please note that they should write our V.A.T. number [quote number] on the outside of all packages and parcels to avoid delay at customs.

Selling through the post

In all advertisements it is wise to state terms and conditions for selling your stamps through the post. For example:

> Send cash with order. All items are offered, subject unsold, on seven days approval against cash paid in advance. All orders under £10 please add extra 20p, on all orders over £10 we will pay postage, packing and insurance. Will all overseas clients please note that they should add extra to remittance to cover registered postage, or registered air mail postage. [To deter any would-be robbers you could add:] Stock not held at these premises.

Capital Gains Tax

At present there is no Capital Gains Tax to pay on any individual stamp sold for under one thousand pounds (£1,000).

V.A.T.

Value Added Tax on stamps over one hundred years old is included in the net price charged by dealers. Under a special V.A.T. scheme (shown below), tax is chargeable only on the margin by which the selling price of the article exceeds its purchase price, i.e. purchase a stamp in 1977 for £150·00, sell that stamp in 1978 for £200·00, and the margin by which the selling price of the article exceeds its purchase price (gross profit) will be £50·00. The current rate of V.A.T. is then paid on that amount.

Stamps under one hundred years old do not come under the scope of the scheme; for these stamps, the current rate of V.A.T. (at present 8 per cent) has to be added to the price.

Many of today's stamp dealers were once ordinary collectors. It probably started as a hobby, but then shrewd buying and selling helped to transform the hobby into a money-making concern. It is only one small leap from a highly profitable pastime to the start of a profitable business. The Customs and Excise V.A.T. office states (at the time of writing) that if the turnover of a hobby/pastime/part-time business exceeds £10,000 p.a. then the person dealing in such activities will be required to register for V.A.T. purposes. Turnover is defined as the total value of sales, not just on the margin of profit.

Listed below are some of the points from the V.A.T. notice dealing with second-hand works of art, antiques and scientific collections. Stamps of over 100 years old are eligible as antiques. All full-time dealers who have a turnover exceeding the current limit have to register for V.A.T. and their V.A.T. registration number should be clearly shown on all letterheads, brochures, etc.

Your attention is drawn to the 'Records to be Kept' section, and in particular the 'Failure to Comply' paragraph in the following notes which are extracts from Notice 712, H.M. Customs & Excise. If you would like to know more about V.A.T. you are advised to contact your local V.A.T. office for detailed and up-to-date advice.

V.A.T. is normally chargeable on the full value of goods sold by a taxable person. But for second-hand works of art, antiques and scientific collections, there is a special scheme whereby, subject to certain conditions, tax is chargeable only on the margin by which the selling price of the article exceeds its purchase price. The special scheme may be operated by a dealer registered for V.A.T. (referred to in this notice as a registered dealer) or by any other taxable person who acquires a second-hand work of art, antique or scientific collection in specified circumstances and sells it in the course of his business, provided that he has not claimed and will not claim deduction of input tax for it.

The first sale of a work of art by its creator and the sale of previously unsold works that form part of his estate are not eligible to be dealt with under the scheme. They are therefore liable to V.A.T. on the full value.

Although tax may be charged on the margin only, taxable turnover for VAT registration purposes (see Notice No. 700, *V.A.T.: General guide*) must include the total value (exclusive of tax) of sales of works of art, antiques and scientific collections. Thus a person who deals in or disposes of works of art, antiques or scientific collections will need to register if his total turnover from their sale or disposal, together with any other taxable turnover, will exceed £10,000 a year.

Nothing in this Notice overrides the legal requirements in the Finance Act 1972 and Orders and Regulations made under that Act (in particular the Value Added Tax (Special Provisions) Order 1977, Statutory Instrument 1977 No. 1796). Except as provided in this Notice the general requirements of Notice No. 700 apply.

Scope of the scheme

The scheme covers the sale of second-hand works of art, antiques and scientific collections, provided that all the following conditions are met.

(a) The article being sold must have been acquired by the taxable seller either: –
   (I) before 1 April 1973; or
   (II) from a non-taxable person; or
   (III) from a taxable person who was not required to account for tax on its full value and did not issue a tax invoice for the supply, i.e. from a person who himself sold the article under this scheme; or
   (IV) by importation under conditions which

relieve it from tax on importation (see imports).

(b) The seller must not have claimed and will not claim deduction of input tax in respect of his acquisition of the article.

(c) The article must not be sold on an invoice showing V.A.T. separately (a tax invoice).

(d) The seller must comply with general conditions explained in this Notice or otherwise required by Customs and Excise.

Articles that meet these conditions are referred to in this Notice as 'eligible articles'.

No deduction of input tax can be claimed for the purchase of any eligible articles sold under the scheme, and the seller need not disclose his margin to the buyer. The information which must be recorded on a sales invoice is shown in Appendix B.

An eligible article may, however, be sold outside the scheme, under the normal tax arrangements, if the seller and the buyer so wish. Tax would then be chargeable on the full value of the sale, a tax invoice would be issued, and the buyer, if he were registered as a taxable person, could claim deductions of input tax subject to the normal rules. The taxable buyer would, however, be required to account for tax on the full value if he later resold the article.

Information and statements on invoices

When a taxable person buys an article from someone who does not issue an invoice, and proposes to resell it under this scheme, the buyer must himself prepare an invoice showing the information in Appendix B. The seller must certify on the invoice that he is the seller at the stated price, sign and date the certificate, and add his address. If it is more convenient, the certificate may be given in a separate document or letter, provided that this is cross-referenced to the invoice. The buyer must certify on the invoice that he is the buyer of the article, and sign and date the certificate. When an article is sold under the scheme the seller must issue an invoice to the buyer showing the information in Appendix B. The seller must keep a copy of the invoice, certifying on it that:

'Input tax deduction has not been and will not be

claimed by me in respect of the goods sold on this invoice'

and sign and date the certificate. Normally the copy sales invoice must also contain a signed and dated certificate by the buyer that he is the buyer of the article at the stated price. But if, exceptionally (e.g. for a sale conducted by correspondence or telephone), the buyer's signature on the invoice cannot be obtained, this certificate may be omitted, provided that the seller can otherwise satisfy Customs and Excise that the article was sold for the stated price to the person whose name and address are shown on the invoice.

When more than one article is sold on the same invoice, a value must be allocated to each article. These values must be identical in the sales records of the seller and the purchase records of the buyer, if both are registered for V.A.T. Similarly, if a collection is acquired as a single unit, and broken up for sale in parts, each part must be allocated a specific part of the total requisition value.

The description of antiques on the invoices must include details of any marks, hall-marks, etc. substantiating their age or a statement that they are over 100 years old.

A registered dealer must cross-reference cash purchases or sales invoice to the stock number in the stock book and to the relevant folio of any day book.

Sales by auction

A taxable person selling an eligible article under the scheme by auction will have to tell the auctioneer that he is doing so and give him the identifying details of the article as in Appendix B. Where the auctioneer renders an invoice in his own name to the buyer, he should deal with the transaction as if it were a sale by an unregistered person under the procedure described in Notice No. 710 (V.A.T.: Supplies by or through agents). That is, he will for V.A.T. purposes record the acquisition and disposal of the article as though he had himself bought it and sold it without profit at the final bid price to the buyer at auction, with no tax involved in either case.

After the sale the auctioneer will have to give the seller

an account showing all the details in Appendix B, which the seller will treat as his sales invoice and deal with as explained in paragraph above. If it is more convenient the identifying details of the article may be omitted from the account, provided that the account is clearly cross-referenced to another document giving those details: e.g. if the details are shown in an auction sale catalogue, the account may simply show the lot number, provided that both the auctioneer and the seller keep copies of the catalogue.

The buyer also, if he is a taxable person, will need an invoice from the auctioneer showing the details in Appendix B in order to be able to resell the article under the scheme. The alternative procedure explained above for giving the details may be used if desired.

The auctioneer must charge tax on his commission and give the seller a tax invoice in respect of it. The seller may treat this tax as deductible input tax, subject to the normal rules and exceptions explained in Notice No. 700 and in Notice No. 706 (V.A.T. Partial exemption).

See also 'exports'.

Gifts

If a taxable person sells an eligible article which he has received as a gift, he must charge tax on its full selling price.

Part exchange

In a part exchange there are in effect two separate supplies at separate prices, i.e. the amount that would be payable for the principal supply if nothing was taken in part exchange and the amount allowed for the goods taken in part exchange. If a registered dealer sells eligible articles and accepts others, or ineligible articles, in part exchange, the gross selling price (inclusive of any tax chargeable) to be entered in the stock book must include the value he allows on the goods taken in part exchange, i.e. that value must be added to the net price (inclusive of any tax chargeable) of the article he is selling. If other eligible articles are taken in part exchange, they must be entered as separate items in the receipts part of the stock book, and the values allowed for these must be shown as their purchase prices.

When a part exchange transaction is entered into with a person who does not issue an invoice, the registered buyer must create a sales invoice on behalf of the seller. It should contain the information in Appendix B and bear a signed and dated certificate from the seller that he is the seller of the article at the stated price.

Deductible input tax

Although the scheme does not permit deduction of input tax to be claimed for the purchase of eligible articles, tax charged to the seller for business overheads, cleaning, restoration, etc. may be deducted in the normal way.

Imports

Antiques and scientific collections covered by the scheme are relieved of tax on importation.

Eligible articles imported by post

A registered taxable person importing eligible articles in the course of his business is strongly advised to arrange for the overseas sender to quote the importer's V.A.T. registration number on the Customs declaration accompanying the package.

Exports

Exports are zero-rated. A registered dealer or other taxable person will not, therefore, need to charge V.A.T. when he exports eligible articles, provided that he fulfils the general conditions in Notice No. 703 (V.A.T.: Exports) or Notice No. 704 (V.A.T.: Retail export schemes).

When an eligible article is sold at auction for export, on behalf of a seller who is a registered dealer or other taxable person, the seller may zero-rate the supply, provided that he holds an appropriate certificate of export supplied by the auctioneer in one of the forms detailed in Appendix D.

Records to be kept

In addition to the records required by Notice No. 700 as modified by this Notice, registered dealers and auctioneers of eligible articles must keep a stock book or similar record showing the information in Appendix C. The description to be recorded in Part A of the stock record must be sufficiently detailed to identify the individual article and, for antiques, it must include the details indicated in paragraph headed 'Information and Statements on Invoices' concerning their age.

Other taxable persons selling goods under the scheme must keep sufficient records to establish readily the margin, if any, on the sale of each article.

Records including purchase and sales invoices and stock books, must be preserved for three years.

If a taxable person fails to comply with this paragraph or with any other condition of this Notice, he may be held accountable for tax on the value of his sales.

Completion of form V.A.T. 100

The return Form V.A.T. 100 is illustrated in Appendix C of Notice 700. The output tax (item 1 on the form) should include the total tax on all eligible articles sold in the period covered by the return, i.e. the total of the amounts in column 13 of the specimen stock book in Appendix C of this Notice. The values to be recorded in Part B of the return against items 11, 12 and 17 are as follows: –

Items 11 and 12	The figure to be inserted must include the total tax-exclusive value of the sales of all eligible articles in the period covered by the return, i.e. the total of column 10 minus column 13 of Appendix C.
Item 17	The figure to be inserted must include the total value (inclusive of any tax) of the purchases of all eligible articles in the period covered by the return, i.e. the total of column 9 of Appendix C.

Appendix B

Information to be shown on invoices

1. Identifying number of invoice.
2. Seller's name and address and V.A.T. registration number, if any.
3. Date of transaction.
4. Buyer's name and address.
5. Description of article (*including, for antiques, age details*).
6. Gross price inclusive of V.A.T. and, if paid wholly or partly by the exchange of other goods, the identifying details of those goods and the amount allowed for them.

Appendix C

Stock book of second-hand works of art, antiques and scientific collections

Specimen layout

PART A	PART B	PART C
Receipts (Columns 1–5)	Disposals (Columns 6–8)	Accounts (Columns 9–13)

Information to be shown

Part A

1. Stock number in numerical sequence.
2. Date of purchase.
3. Purchase invoice number.
4. Seller's name and address.
5. Description of the article (including, for antiques, age details).

Part B

6. Date of sale.
7. Sales invoice number.
8. Buyer's name and address.

Part C

9. Purchase price (inclusive of any tax).
10. Gross selling price (inclusive of any tax), or method of disposal if not sold.
11. Margin on sale – item 10 less item 9.
12. Tax rate at time of sale.
13. Tax on margin due to Customs and Excise.

Appendix D

Certificates of export for goods sold at auction

Provided that he holds evidence of the export of articles sold at his auction, an auctioneer may provide the registered dealer or other taxable person who offered the articles for sale with a signed and dated certificate of export of one of the following forms, as appropriate: –

(a) For goods exported direct by the auctioneer by sea or by air (See Notice No. 703, V.A.T.: Exports, Section 11)

I .... (full name of signatory) certify that the article(s) detailed below and sold as Lot No(s) .... at auction by me on .... (date of sale) has/have* been exported on the undermentioned vessel/aircraft*: –
Description of article(s) ....
Name of export vessel, or aircraft flight prefix and number ....
Port or airport of loading ....
Date of sailing or departure ....
Bill of lading or air waybill number (where appropriate) ....
Identifying number of container or railway wagon (if

used) ....
.... (Signature of auctioneer)
Date.................
* Delete as necessary.
   (b) For goods exported direct by the auctioneer by
       post (See Notice No. 703, V.A.T.: Exports, Sec-
       tion IV)
I .... (full
name of signatory) certify that the article(s) detailed
below and sold as Lot No(s) .... at auction by me
on .... (date of sale) has/have* been
exported by me by post on .... (date
of posting). A certificate/certificates* of posting is/are*
held.
   Description of article(s)
        .... (Signature of auctioneer)
        Date.................
* Delete as necessary.
   (c) For goods disposed of under the retail export
       schemes (See Notice No. 704, V.A.T.: Retail
       Export Schemes, Sections II and III)
I .... (full
name of signatory) certify that the article(s) detailed
below and sold as Lot No(s) .... at auction by me
on .... (date of sale) have been
exported under the Personal Export Scheme/Over-the-
Counter Scheme*. The appropriate Form V.A.T. 408/
409 or 413/414 completed by Customs and Excise, is held.
   Description of article(s)
        .... (Signature of auctioneer)
        Date.................
* Delete as necessary.

The above extracts are from V.A.T. Notice No. 712 as it
affects stamp dealers and collectors. To study the whole
question of V.A.T. you are advised to obtain a copy of
Notice 712 plus all the other notices mentioned in the
above text.

Accountants

For the serious, and successful collector/investor there can
be a fair amount of bookwork to do. If you intend to make

stamp collecting a profitable pastime, a part-time business, or eventually a full-time occupation, you are advised to get a good accountant to deal with your tax. If your turnover exceeds the V.A.T. limit, then V.A.T. registration will apply to you and the same conditions for registration will apply to you as they do for a dealer. In fact you will become 'a registered dealer'. A good accountant can save you a lot of time and trouble, as well as getting all the various allowances for you.

The philatelic society you join can probably give you a contact number for any accountants interested in philately. It is best to go and interview several accountants before making up your mind. An accountant whom you can get on with could prove, in time, to be a good friend and advisor.

Tax and national insurance

Whether or not you think it necessary to take on an accountant, it is your job to let the local tax inspector know, on form 41G, if you operate a financially rewarding sideline. The Department of Health and Social Security also need to know if you are working partly for yourself, and also for an employer, because this may affect your National Insurance contributions.

Registering a business name

If you decide to trade under a name other than your own, you will have to apply to: Registrar of Business Names, Pembroke House, 40–56 City Road, London EC1Y 2DN. This regulation comes under the Registration of Business Names Act 1916. Even if you use the words 'stamps' or 'philately' after your own name, you must still register.

Limited company

If you build up a sizeable business you could think about forming a limited company. Your accountant, or solicitor can advise you about this, or you can contact a company registration agency in London. See the Yellow Pages telephone directory which covers the London area, in particular, the City area, or have a look at the *Exchange & Mart* for a list of these company registration and formation agencies.

12 PHILATELIC TERMS

ABNORMALS: Stamps produced from plates which were not originally intended for that purpose. Examples of these are some of the Victorian stamps.

ADHESIVE: The name given to any postage stamp which is coated with gum on the reverse.

AEROGRAMME: A light-weight sheet of notepaper specially produced for airmail postage at a reduced rate of postage.

AERO-PHILATELY: The term used for the study of airmail postage and its associations.

ALBINO: A stamp having no inking, which has been released in error, and is colourless.

ALPHABET: Certain letters used in the printing of stamps which help to identify certain sets because of the particular types of lettering.

ANILINE: A chemical fluid used to produce brilliantly coloured stamps.

APO: Army Post Office.

APPROVALS: Stamps sent out by a dealer to a customer so that the latter can study them before purchasing.

ARROW BLOCK: A sheet of stamps which has arrows printed in the margin. These act as a guide in dividing the sheet.

AS IS: The term used at auctions when no guarantee is given.

BACKPRINT: Print on the reverse of stamps.

BACKSTAMP: A postmark usually recording the receipt of a piece of mail, normally hand-stamped on the reverse.

BALLON MONTÉ: The stamp used on mail carried by a piloted balloon during the Paris siege. If the mail was carried by an unarmed balloon, the words 'Ballon non-monté' were used.

BANTAMS: Miniature stamps issued by South Africa during World War Two, in an attempt to save paper.

BAR CANCELLATIONS: Heavy bars printed on stamps to indicate that they have been cancelled and are not therefore valid for postal use.

BÂTONNÉ PAPER: Paper which has wide watermarked guide-lines.

BILINGUAL: One stamp printed in two languages.

BILINGUAL PAIR: Two similar stamps, adjoined and printed each in a different language, e.g. English and Afrikaans.

BIOT: British Indian Ocean Territories.

BISECT: A stamp which has been officially cut in half, in any direction, and worth half the original denomination.

BISHOP MARK: The date stamp introduced in 1661 by Henry Bishop.

BLEUTÉ PAPER: Paper which has a bluish tone.

BLIND PERFORATION: An indented line on a stamp in place of the perforations. This is where the perforator struck the paper but failed to produce perforations.

BLOCK: Stamps joined to form a rectangle, made up from four or more.

BNA: British North America.

BOGUS: A stamp issued illegally by an individual; also the term given to a genuine stamp which has an unauthorized overprint.

BOÎTE MOBILE: Mail box on ships or ferries used during a voyage.

BOOKLET: A small book of stamps usually containing several denominations.

BOOKLET PANE: A page showing some or all the denominations of a stamp booklet, plus advertisements, etc.

BOTH SIDES: Used when referring to stamps which are printed on both sides and which differ from set-offs in that the impression is not in reverse, but reads the correct way.

BOXED: The term used when a postmark is surrounded by a rectangular frame.

BULL'S EYES: A nickname given to Brazilian stamps of 1843, because of their design.

BUREAU PRINT: Stamps which have been pre-cancelled by the American Bureau of Engraving and Printing before they are issued.

BURELAGE: A pattern of fine wavy lines or dots which often forms the base of a stamp design, and is sometimes printed on the reverse. A form of security printing.

BWI: British West Indies.

C: In the scale of stamp rarity, C stands for Common.

CA: Crown Agents.

CACHET: A type of postmark, usually made by a hand-stamp, but sometimes in the form of a label or printed design, often used on first issues, or to mark some special occasion.

CANCELLATION: A mark made on a stamp to show that it is invalid for further postal use. A cancellation mark can be made by a postmark or by pen.

CANCELLATION TO COMPLAISANCE: The term used when stamps are specially postmarked for collectors.

CANCELLATION-TO-ORDER: Stamps postmarked without having been used on postage. This is often done by governments when there is a surplus of old stock. The stamps are then offered by the trade, very often in small packets for beginners.

CANTONAL STAMPS: Stamps which were issued by the Cantons of Geneva, Basle and Zürich. These were the first Swiss stamps.

CARLIST: Stamps named after Don Carlos and issued by him in 1873–4. He was the Spanish Pretender.

CARNET: The French word for stamp booklet.

CARRIERS' STAMPS: Stamps which were delivered by independent letter carriers in the United States, in areas where no official government services were operating. The carriers often issued their own stamps, and sometimes the postmasters of the contact offices issued special carrier stamps.

CAT: The value as stated in any particular catalogue.

CATALOGUE: The official price lists issued by various philatelic companies giving relevant details of the stamps offered for sale, such as perforations, colours, etc. The prices quoted are generally used for assessing the value of any particular stamp.

CC: Crown Colony. Also colour changes. (If the colour of succeeding issues differ from the original issue.)

CDS: Circular date stamp.

CEMENT: A term used to describe the gum of early British stamps.

CENSOR MARK: A mark made by a censor on mail, usually military and civil.

CENTRED: A term used to describe the exact location of the design of a stamp within the boundaries of the four perforations. A perfectly centred stamp is one where the design lies exactly in the centre of the stamp. If a stamp is described as off-centre, it means that the sheet has not been perfectly perforated, and that, therefore, the margins surrounding the stamps are of different breadths. If a stamp is said to be centred to the top it means that the main central design lies more to the top of the area of stamp than to the bottom; therefore, there would be a wider margin along the bottom perforations.

CHALK LINES: A method of deterring counterfeiters, used in Russia at the start of the century, whereby crisscross lines of a chalky substance were laid under the design.

CHALKY PAPER: Paper with a chalky surface used for making stamps. Because the surface is easily smudged, it makes it difficult to pass off stamps made of this paper as being unused. They could not, therefore, be re-used for postage.

CHALON HEAD: The name given to stamps of the West Indies, Natal and New Zealand etc. which have a design of Queen Victoria as painted by A. E. Chalon.

CHANGELING: The term used when the colour of a stamp has changed, either by accident, such as by sunlight, or by fraud.

CHARITY STAMP: A stamp which is sold by the postal authorities at a higher price than that on the face. The extra income from such stamps is then donated to a particular charity, which is usually depicted on the stamp.

CHECK LETTERS: Small letters which were printed in the corners of early British stamps to assist in locating their positions on the sheet. A double lettering system was used so that every stamp contained a different pair of letters.

CIGARETTE PAPER: Very thin paper of the type used for making cigarettes.

CLASSIC: The term used to describe the first issues of any particular country. All the early stamps of the world.

CLEANED STAMP: A stamp which has been chemically treated to remove the cancellation marks. These are sometimes used for postage, and are often offered to the trade with a forged postmark.

CLICHÉ: The name given to the design block of a stamp-printing plate.

COATED: A stamp which has been made from paper bearing a special coating, such as chalk.

COIL: The term used for stamps which have been issued in a long roll, of the type used in vending machines. Sometimes these are referred to as rolls of stamps.

COLLEGE STAMPS: The name given to stamps which were

used between 1871 and 1886 on mail from Oxford and Cambridge. These stamps were specially produced for the college-messenger system.

COLOUR TRIALS: Stamps which are produced in proof form in several different colours so that a final colour can be selected for the issue.

COLUMN: The vertical row of stamps on a sheet.

COMB PERF: Perforations produced by a machine which acts in a combing motion and perforates the top and two sides of each stamp in the row in one sweep. The stamps are then moved up one place, and with the second sweep the machine repeats the action of perforating the top and two sides of the second row of stamps, thus adding the bottom perforations to the first row of stamps, and so on until the sheet has been completely perforated.

COMBINATION COVER: A cover which contains the stamps of more than one country, mostly used on early mail which had geographical restrictions placed on it by the issuing authorities, and had therefore to be complemented by additional stamps of neighbouring authorities. This term is sometimes used to describe covers bearing stamps of different denominations.

COMMEMORATIVE: A stamp specially issued to commemorate an anniversary or a special occasion.

COMPOUND PERF.: A term used to denote that the perforations on a stamp are not the same on all four sides.

CONDOMINIUM: Used when a territory is ruled by more than one authority.

CONTROL LETTERS: Letters or numbers (in some cases both) printed in the margin of stamp sheets giving indications as to the date, accounting period, etc.

COPPER PLATE: Sometimes abbreviated to CP, this is used to show that stamps have been produced by the copper-plate method.

CORK CANCELLATIONS: A method of cancelling mail by means of a cork. Used at times when a normal stamp was unobtainable. Sometimes cork hand-stamps were used to obliterate certain details on stamps, but this was usually an official practice in times of unrest such as war in any particular nation.

CORNER BLOCK: The section of a sheet of stamps from one of the corners which still has the corner margin attached, and probably also some control numbers, etc. printed on

87

the margin. Often corner blocks may differ in some respect from the stamps on the rest of the sheet.

COVER: The complete envelope or wrapper to which the stamp has been stuck for postage. Sometimes stamps are offered with only part of the envelope attached; these are known as 'on piece'. If the entire cover is offered with the stamp attached, the term used is 'on original cover' or sometimes 'on entire'.

C-T-O: The letters which stand for 'Cancellation-to-Order' as described above.

CUBIERTAS: The name given to large labels of declaration which are used on mail of the Columbian states.

CURRENT NUMBER: A number shown in the margin of stamp sheets indicating the printer's plate sequence.

CUT-OUTS: Stamps which have been previously printed and impressed on postal stationery, and are cut out and used with glue for postal purposes, or mounted for display.

CUT SQUARE: Stamps which have been cut out from postal stationery in a square or rectangle, and not from the exact border of the design which could have been round or oval.

CYLINDER BLOCK: The corner block of stamps in a sheet attached to the margin showing the cylinder numbers.

CYLINDER NUMBER: The number entered on the margin of a sheet indicating the cylinder used in the printing. If a stamp had, say, five different colours, there would be five different cylinder numbers shown on the margin, each representing a different colour. Used on photogravure stamps.

DANDY ROLL: A cylinder containing the watermark design, used in the manufacture of paper.

DATESTAMP: The mark made on mail by means of a hand- or machine-operated stamp which prints the date.

DEFACED PLATE: A printing plate which has been altered in some way so as to prevent further stamps being run off after an issue has been completed.

DEFINITIVE ISSUES: The usual design for any particular country's stamps which are printed in all denominations and are the standard issue of that country, apart from commemoratives etc. Very often definitives bear the head of the sovereign.

DELACRYL: De La Rue & Co. method of printing by lithography.

88

DEMONETIZED: Stamps which are no longer valid for postal use.

DENOMINATION: The face value of a stamp.

DENTELÉ: The French term for perforated.

DEPARTMENTALS: Stamps which have been used exclusively by the inter-governmental departments, particularly in America.

DES: An abbreviation for the words 'designed by'.

DESULPHURATE: A process of removing a build-up of sulphur from the surface of stamps which have suffered a deterioration in colour. The original colour can be restored by treating them with a solution of hydrogen peroxide.

DICKINSON PAPER: A special paper invented by a man named John Dickinson, which has a continuous silk thread running through it. This paper was used to produce Mulready envelopes.

DIE: The piece of metal which has been engraved with the pattern for the stamps, from which the plate copies are taken.

DIE PROOF: The sample of a particular design produced from the original die. This is usually produced in black ink on a white surface, and it is inspected for errors before authority can be given to use the die for an issue of stamps.

DISINFECTED: In some countries where there was danger of disease being spread by mail, postal matter was disinfected by the authorities. This was often the case during plague or other epidemics.

DOCKWRA MARK: A postmark introduced by William Dockwra in the year 1680 to show that postage had been paid. These marks were triangular in shape.

DOCTOR BLADE: The blade which is used to clean surplus ink from the cylinder during the printing of photogravure stamps. A doctor blade flaw is caused when the blade fails to operate perfectly, and this is recognizable by a thin line of deeper colour or white running across the stamp.

DOMINICAL LABEL: The label which was attached to mail bearing Belgian stamps between 1893 and 1914, instructing the postal authorities that the mail was not to be delivered on Sundays.

DOUBLE IMPRESSION: Stamps which have been printed twice, thus giving a double design. This is caused when the paper is not properly placed in the printing machine, or sometimes when a sheet is run through in error after it has already been printed.

DOUBLE PERFORATION: Stamps which have two rows of perforations along any one of the four sides.

DROP LETTER: A letter which is both received and delivered by the same post office, i.e. in the same village or town.

DRY PRINT: A stamp which has a very faint covering of ink but whose colour is still recognizable. This should not be confused with an albino, which has no ink at all.

DUES: The nickname given to mail on which postage is due, or to postage-due stamps.

DUMB CANCELLATIONS: A method of cancelling mail with no trace of the place of origin showing. This method was used extensively during the war in order to keep the location of the sender secret.

DUPLEX CANCELLATION: A method of cancellation which was used during the reign of Queen Victoria. This had a circular town mark, also an adjoining mark bearing the number representing the particular town shown on the mark.

DUTY PLATE: The printing plate bearing the denomination when the main design of the stamp is printed from a different standard plate.

ELECTRIC EYE: A perforating system which produces perfect sheets.

EMBOSSED: Stamps which have been printed with the main design in relief.

ENCASED: Stamps which were specially enclosed or protected in a case and which were exchanged as currency. The casing was intended to lengthen the life of the stamp.

ENG: Abbreviation for engraved.

ENGINE-TURNED: The term used when stamps are produced bearing a complex background pattern which is produced by a machine called a Rose-engine, after the man who invented it.

ENGRAVED: Also referred to as line-engraved, this indicates that the stamps have been produced by means of plates engraved in recess.

ENTIRE: The term used when referring to complete postcards, letters, envelopes or wrappings which contain the stamp plus any other labels, etc. and which are preserved intact.

ERROR: A stamp which contains an inaccuracy in the

design, colour, inscription, watermark, etc. This should not be confused with a variety, which is only slightly different from the main issue.

ESSAY: A proposed design for a stamp which has been rejected by the authorities.

EST: Abbreviation for estimated price.

EXCHANGE CLUB: A club formed by individuals who participate in stamp dealing by means of the circulating packet.

EXPERT COMMITTEES: Special recognized committees are set up by leading philatelic organizations in order to establish whether or not certain stamps are genuine. They issue an official certificate bearing their comments and also a photograph of the stamp in question.

EXPLODED: The term used when referring to the pages of stamp booklets when they have been separated for display.

EXPRESS: Stamps which have been issued particularly for use on express delivery mail.

EXTENSION PERF HOLE: The length (or number of holes) by which the line of perforations has extended into the margin.

FACE: The surface of the stamp opposite to the gummed reverse on which is shown the design.

FACE VALUE: The amount of money which the stamp is worth for postage.

FACSIMILE: A fake stamp, but one which is recognized as such because of the overprint 'facsimile'; these are often marketed as collectors' items.

FAKE: A stamp which has been illegally altered to appear different, and often more valuable; not to be confused with errors and varieties, which are officially issued.

FDC: First day cover. A stamp which has come from a new issue (first day) and is still attached to the cover.

FIP: The initials of the Fédération Internationale de Philatélie, the international philatelic organization.

FIRST FLIGHT: Cards and covers carried on the first flight of an airmail route.

FISCAL: A stamp which is not of the postage variety.

FLAW: An irregularity caused by a damaged printing plate or cylinder. Sometimes the irregularity starts off by a faint marking on the surface of the stamps, then as the print-run progresses, the marks become more distinguishable.

FLOWN COVER: A cover which bears evidence that it has been delivered by means of airmail procedure.

FLYSPECK: The term used when a tiny particle of matter on the printing plate has shown up on the stamps. It is also used in a derisive sense.

FORGERY: An illegally produced stamp.

FPO: Abbreviations for Field Post Office, used by servicemen on active duty in the field.

FRAME: The border of a stamp, sometimes in elaborate design, and sometimes printed in a plain colour.

FRANK: Originally this term was applied when referring to a signature or personal stamp which certain parties and privileged individuals placed on their mail to denote that the letters were to be despatched free of charge. Also the stamping of mail by franking machines, which denotes that the mail has been prepaid.

FRESH: Term used to describe a stamp which is in good condition with emphasis on the colour.

FRONT: That part of a cover which shows the postmark and the stamp, as well as any other labels, etc. cut away from the body of the cover.

FU: Abbreviation for Fine Used.

FUGITIVE: Stamps made from special ink which runs when moisture is placed in contact, therefore making it difficult to remove postmarks, etc.

GAUGE: The number of teeth or holes in the perforation along any side of the stamp within a length of 20 mm. Also the instrument of measurement.

GENERAL COLLECTION: A collection of stamps which includes stamps of all countries, and which is not thematic or specialist.

GPO: General Post Office.

GRANITE PAPER: Paper which contains minute hairs or fibres which can be easily seen.

GRAPHITE LINES: Lines on the reverse of British stamps which were of graphite and conductive. The lines were printed on the reverse under the coating of gum, and these stamps were used in conjunction with an electronic sorting machine in 1957.

GRILL: Embossed dots on stamps of Peru and America, which broke the surface of the paper when postmarked, thus allowing the ink to penetrate into the paper, making it difficult if not impossible to remove the cancellation.

GUARANTEE MARK: A mark made on the reverse of some stamps by certain dealers who have their own distinctive marks. This shows that the stamp is guaranteed to be genuine.

GUIDE LINES: Lines made on the plate in order to guide the printer. If these are not properly removed, traces can be seen on the stamps, usually very close to the frame. Sometimes dots are used instead of lines.

GUILLOTINE PERFORATION: A method of producing perforations by one action of the machine, similar to the action of a guillotine, whereby the holes fall in one long straight line.

GUM: The adhesive substance on the reverse of mint stamps which when moistened becomes activated, and thus allows the stamp to be stuck on to the cover.

GUTTERS: The spaces between the panes of stamps in a sheet.

HAIRLINES: Very fine lines on stamps which can either be coloured lines on the unprinted area or vice versa.

HAND-STAMP: A mark made on an item of postage by hand rather than by machine.

HAND-STRUCK: A stamp which has been made from a hand-operated die as opposed to a machine-operated die.

HARROW PERFORATION: A perforation system which perforates an entire sheet of stamps in one action.

HEALTH STAMPS: Charity stamps of Fiji and New Zealand, bearing a premium which is used to help underprivileged children.

HEAVY CANCEL: A method of completely obliterating the design of a stamp by over-inking.

HINGE: A small gummed piece of paper which is used for mounting stamps in albums.

HOTEL STAMPS: Stamps which were issued privately by hotels, mostly in Switzerland. These stamps were attached to mail for despatch from the hotel to the nearest post office.

IMPERFORATE: A stamp which has to be cut from the sheet because there have been no perforations.

IMPRIMATUR: A stamp from the sheets which were registered at Somerset House, and which had to be cut away from the sheet because they were produced as imperforate, although the actual stamps issued did contain perforations.

IMPRINT: The name of the printer, or sometimes his mark, on a sheet of stamps.

INTAGLIO: A term used when referring to engraving in recess.

INTERRUPTED PERFORATION: This method of producing coils of stamps for vending machines was introduced to strengthen the rolls by omitting some of the perforation holes.

INVALIDATED: Stamps which cannot be used for postal purposes because they have been rendered invalid.

INVERTED: Upside down.

IVORY HEAD: British stamps of 1841 which show a white head on the reverse due to a chemical reaction in the blueing of the paper.

JOURNAL STAMP: Postage stamps which were specially printed for use on journals and newspapers.

JUBILEE LINE: The Jubilee of Queen Victoria saw the issue of stamps bearing bordering lines that were caused by the printer's rule which was placed on the plate to prevent wear.

KEY PLATE: The plate from which the main design and border is taken for stamps. A key plate can contain additional details such as different postal duties or territories.

KILLER: A very heavy cancellation mark which normally obliterates the entire design.

KILOWARE: Bags of assorted stamps weighing a kilogram and sold at a flat rate.

KNIFE: The name given to an envelope before it is folded.

LAID PAPER: Paper containing criss-cross watermarked lines, the lines in one direction being close together, and the lines in the other direction, more widely spaced.

LINE ENGRAVED: Another name for intaglio or recess printing as described above.

LOCALS: Stamps specially issued to be used in a restricted area.

LOOSE-LEAF ALBUMS: Stamp albums containing loose leaves as opposed to the type where the pages are permanently bound and pre-printed.

M: Mint.

MALTESE CROSS: Cancellations or obliterations in the shape of a Maltese Cross, also used as a watermark design.

MARGINAL MARKINGS: Any type of instruction or indication

shown in the margin of a stamp sheet, such as control numbers, arrow marks, etc.

MATRIX: An impression from the original die for making exact copies.

MAXIMUM CARDS: A card bearing an illustration of the subject or its associations connected with the issue, stamped and postmarked on the picture side.

METER MARKS: A machine which marks postage items with a postage-paid sign.

MINIATURE SHEET: A very small sheet with wide margins bearing one to four stamps, usually thematic or commemorative.

MINT: A stamp which is in perfect condition, unused and unaltered from the condition in which it left the printer.

MOUNT: A device for attaching stamps to album pages, such as a hinge.

MULREADY: Envelopes designed by William Mulready in 1840, which were prepaid.

MULTIPLE: The term used to describe three or more adjoining stamps.

MULTIPLE WATERMARKS: A method of watermarking introduced in Great Britain in 1904, whereby the designs in the watermark are repeated.

NH: Abbreviation for never hinged.

O: Abbreviation for ordinary, when referring to the type of paper used in the printing of stamps.

OBLITERATOR: A machine or hand-stamp used to cancel stamps.

OBSOLETE: The stamp can no longer be purchased at the Post Office.

OFF-CENTRE: A term used when referring to a stamp which has not been perfectly centred between the margins.

OFFICIALS: Stamps used by government departments, often normal stamps which have been overprinted.

OG: Abbreviation for original gum.

OMNIBUS ISSUES: A group of issues produced by various countries at the same time, usually to mark a special occasion such as a coronation. The stamps are similar.

ON PIECE: Used when a stamp is attached to a piece of the cover rather than the entire cover.

OVERPRINT: Any additional print on a stamp made after

the original printing. Any part of the stamp except the denomination is called an overprint; the denomination when altered becomes the surcharge.

PACKET BOAT: Ships which were specially contracted to transport mail.

PANE: The areas of stamps on a sheet which are separated from the others by means of a gutter.

PAQUEBOT: The name given to the cancellation of mail posted aboard ships.

PATRIOTIC COVERS: Propaganda covers used by the Union and Confederacy during the American Civil War.

PC: Postcard.

PELURE: A type of very thin brittle paper.

PEN CANCELLED: Rare stamps which have been cancelled by pen by the postmaster, usually in urgent circumstances.

PERF: Perforated.

PERFIN: A stamp which bears the initials of the company in perforation marks across the centre.

PHILATELIST: A person who studies stamps.

PHOSPHOR BAND: Bands on stamps which replace the graphite lines; used in conjunction with an electronic letter-facing machine.

PHOTO: Abbreviation for photogravure.

PIECE: The part of a cover containing the stamp, the postmark and any other marks in connection with the postage.

PL: Abbreviation for plate.

PMK: Abbreviation for postmark.

POACHED EGG: Label used for testing vending machines, and which carry a poached-egg-like pattern.

POSITIONED PIECE: A portion of a sheet of stamps showing the margin and containing marks which can identify the location of a variety from that portion, thus proving it to be genuine. *See also* Testing label.

PPC: Picture postcard.

PRE-ADHESIVE COVERS: Early mail which was despatched before the introduction of adhesive postage stamps.

PRE-CANCELS: Large amounts of stamps sold to a company which have already been cancelled by the authorities, in order to save time.

PRINTED ON GUM: Sometimes stamps are printed on the gummed reverse in error.

PRINTERS' WASTE: Stamps which have leaked through into the market from the printers' defective sheets.

PROOF: A sample or specimen of a new issue which can be carefully studied to ensure that every detail is correct before the stamps are printed for issue.

PROVISIONALS: Stamps which have been overprinted or surcharged by an authority because of short supply, or when required by sudden changes, i.e., a new government in power.

QUADRILLE PAPER: Paper with a background of very faint (often watermarked) lines at right angles. Usually found in loose-leaf albums.

QUARTZ LAMP: An electric lamp which produces ultraviolet rays by using a fused transparent quartz filament. The lamp is used by specialists to examine stamps closely.

R: Abbreviation for reprint.

RECESS PRINTING: Intaglio or line engraved.

RECONSTRUCTION: A sheet of stamps reassembled in much the same way as a jigsaw puzzle, using the corners and marginal instructions as a guide. A reconstruction can contain strips of stamps or can be made entirely from single stamps.

RE-CUT: A term used to describe a die which has been extensively retouched.

RE-DRAWN: A term used to describe a stamp which has minor details redrawn into the design, but which is mainly similar to the original design.

RE-ENTRY: A repair to a damaged design on a plate which has been already used for producing stamps. It shows up as a doubling of that part of the design.

REGIONAL: A stamp issued for use in only part of the territory under the authority of a postal administration.

REMAINDER: A stamp from an issue which has been withdrawn. Such stamps are cancelled-to-order, and sold to the trade.

REPAIR: A corrected flaw in typographical or line-engraved printing.

REPP: A type of heavy paper with fine parallel lines impressed in the surface.

REPRINTS: Stamps officially reprinted by a postal administration to a design similar, or identical, to a classic early issue but often printed on different paper or containing different watermarks or perforations. The original plates are used.

RE-TOUCH: A minor repair to a stamp design, usually detectable.

REVERSED: A mirror image often used when referring to watermarks.

ROLL: Another name for a coil of stamps.

ROULETTE: A form of separation which cuts into the paper but does not leave holes, as in the case of perforation.

ROW: The stamps running horizontally or vertically across or down the sheet.

RUN: The loss of colour produced by fugitive inks when they come into contact with moisture.

S: Abbreviation for specimen or scarce.

ST ANDREW'S CROSS: A cross printed on the blank squares of a stamp booklet where no stamp is issued on that section. The cross prevents forgers using the stamp paper.

SB: Abbreviation for stock book.

SEALS: Charity stickers. Also used to describe stamps issued in Egypt for the British Forces. A special reduction is shown on the stamps.

SELVEDGE: The edging of a sheet, or gutter margin, or pane.

SERVICE OVERPRINT: A stamp specially overprinted for use by military personnel.

SET: A complete issue, covering every denomination printed, or any group of stamps which are related in any way.

SE-TENANT: Two adjoined stamps of different design or colour, divided by a perforation.

SETTING: The location and arrangement of the type used for overprinting.

SG: Abbreviation for Stanley Gibbons.

SHADE: The slight variation of the colour of a stamp, either in depth or tone.

SHIFT: A stamp which has at least one colour off register.

SHIP LETTER: Letters given to a ship's captain for despatch, specially postmarked by the post office of the destination port.

SHORT PERF: A stamp containing a missing tooth on the perforation.

SHORT SET: An incomplete set, usually with the most valuable stamp missing.

SIDE: Abbreviation for sideways watermark.

SIDE-DELIVERY: A term used when coil stamps are issued from a vending machine side by side, as opposed to top to tail.

SINGLE: An individual stamp.

SOUVENIR SHEET: A sheet of stamps issued to mark a special occasion, but which is not always valid for postal use.

SPACE FILLER: Any stamp, e.g. a double or a stamp in poor condition which is mounted in an album in order to fill up a gap, and which will be removed when the correct stamp is obtained.

SPECIMEN: A stamp which is issued by the postal authorities as an example only and is not valid for postal purposes.

SPECULATIVE ISSUES: Stamps issued exclusively for collectors.

STAMP CURRENCY: Stamps substituted for coins, often encased in a protective covering.

STC: Abbreviations for stated to catalogue, when referring to price.

STRAIGHT EDGE: Stamps which have not been perforated on all four sides, such as in the case of coil stamps, or booklet stamps.

STRIKE: The term used to describe the action of a handstamp.

STRIP: Three or more stamps adjoined by perforations belonging to the same row, or column.

SURCHARGE: An overprint which changes the postal duty on a stamp, and sometimes confirms it.

TABS: The border of a sheet of stamps containing additional relevant information, such as inscriptions, etc.

TAGGING: The term used to describe the special treatment given to stamps in order to trigger off an automatic sorting machine, such as in the case of phosphor bands.

TESTING LABEL: Another name for the term poached eggs, applied to the stamps used for testing vending machines for coil stamps. The design on the stamps or testing labels is somewhat similar to poached eggs and thus renders the stamp invalid.

TÊTE BÊCHE: Two stamps joined together with one of them upside down.

THEMATICS: Collecting to a theme or subject, such as ships, trains, plants, etc.

THIN: The term used to describe a stamp which has been damaged on the reverse, probably by careless removal from the cover.

TIED: The term used when a postmark covers part of the stamp and part of the cover. The postmark ties the two together.

TINTED: Paper which is dyed a definite colour.

TONED: Paper which is not dyed, but has a natural tint, usually pale cream, pale brown, or pale blue.

TPO: Abbreviation for travelling post office, usually when referring to the mail train.

TRAINING STAMP: Invalid stamps used for the training of new post-office staff.

TRANSIT MARKS: Marks made on mail while in transit to the destination, such as 'gone-away' notices or redirection, etc.

U: Abbreviation for used.

UM: Abbreviation for unmounted mint.

UN: Abbreviation for unused.

UNCAT: Abbreviation for uncatalogued, meaning not listed in the main catalogues, or, if listed, unpriced.

UNDERPRINT: Markings on the reverse of a stamp usually under the gum, often for protective purposes, and sometimes giving the initials of the organization with exclusive authority to use the stamp.

UNSORTED: A loose mixture of stamps which has not been inspected for valuable stamps, but mostly containing common stamps.

UNUSED: A stamp which is in less than mint condition, yet has never been cancelled.

UPU: Abbreviations for Universal Postal Union which governs international relations for postal services.

USED: A stamp which has been used for postal purposes, as opposed to stamps which have been cancelled-to-order.

USED ABROAD: Stamps of one nation which have been used abroad via a postal administration of the country of origin having been set up abroad.

UV: Abbreviation for ultra-violet, as in test lamps and phosphorus activation.

UW: Abbreviation for unwatermarked.

VALUE TABLET: The area of a stamp containing the denomination.

VARIETY: A stamp which varies from the others in the sheet because it contains a slight inaccuracy, e.g., colour-fade, etc.

VIGNETTE: The main design of a stamp as opposed to the frame or border.

WATERMARK: A transparent mark impressed into the paper during manufacture in order to prevent forgery. An all-over pattern is sometimes used for an entire sheet; or the stamps can be individually watermarked.

WEAK: The term used to describe a stamp which is not in good condition but is not bad enough to be described as damaged. Usually stamps with thinning or curled corners fall into this category.

WMK: Abbreviation for watermark.

WOVE PAPER: Paper which has a woven appearance produced by a watermark made from setting fibres on fine wire mesh.

WRECK COVERS: Mail salvaged from wrecked ships.

WRITING UP: The notes made by a collector in an album giving relevant information about the stamps.

ZEPPELIN STAMPS: Stamps used on mail despatched by Zeppelin airships.

BIBLIOGRAPHY

Books

ANTHONY, Kenneth W., *Beginner's Guide to Stamp Collecting*, Pelham Books, 1971

BATEMAN, Robert, *Specialized Stamp Collecting*, Arthur Barker, 1971

GUNSTON, Bill, *The Philatelist's Companion*, David & Charles, 1975

KEEP, David, *History Through Stamps*, David & Charles, 1974

LAKE, Kenneth R., *Stamps for Investment*, W. H. Allen, 1969

MELVILLE, Fred J., *Stamp Collecting*, The English Universities Press, 1954

NARBETH, Colin, *An Introduction to Stamp Collecting*, Arthur Barker, 1970

NARBETH, Colin, *Beginner's Guide to Stamp Collecting*, Arthur Barker, 1970

NARBETH, Colin, *Collecting British Stamps*, Arthur Barker, 1969

NARBETH, Colin, *Investing in Stamps*, Arthur Barker, 1968

NEW, Anthony, S. B., *The Observer's Book of Postage Stamps*, Frederick Warne & Co., 1967

PEARSON, Patrick, *Advanced Philatelic Research*, Arthur Barker, 1971

PHILLIPS, Stanley, *Stamp Collecting*, Stanley Gibbons, 1975

POTTER, David, *British Elizabethan Stamps*, Batsford, 1971

WATSON, James, *Branching Out in Stamp Collecting*, Arthur Barker, 1970

Catalogues

Stanley Gibbons – British Commonwealth

Stanley Gibbons – Volume I: Europe (Countries A–F)
              – Volume II: Europe (Countries G–P)
              – Volume III: Europe (Countries Q–Z)

Stanley Gibbons – Volume I: Overseas (Countries A–C)
              – Volume II: Overseas (Countries D–J)
              – Volume III: Overseas (Countries K–O)
              – Volume IV: Overseas (Countries P–Z)

Stanley Gibbons Elizabethan

Stanley Gibbons Specialized – Volume I: Queen Victoria
– Volume II: King Edward VII, George V, Edward VIII and George VI
– Volume III: Queen Elizabeth II Pre-decimal Issues
– Volume IV: Queen Elizabeth II Decimal Issues

Commonwealth Catalogue of George VI: Bridger & Kay

Scott 1978 U.S. Specialized Catalogue of United States Stamps by James B. Hatcher, Scott Publishing Company

Magazines

Gibbons Stamp Monthly

Stamp Magazine

Philatelic Magazine

Stamp Collecting Weekly

The Philatelist

The London Philatelist

The Stamp Lover

GPO Philatelic Bulletin